CURRICULUM AND THE AMERICAN RURAL SCHOOL

Doug Feldmann

University Press of America,® Inc.
Lanham · New York · Oxford

Copyright © 2003 by
University Press of America,® Inc.
4501 Forbes Boulevard
Suite 200
Lanham, Maryland 20706
UPA Acquisitions Department (301) 459-3366

PO Box 317
Oxford
OX2 9RU, UK

Library of Congress Cataloging-in-Publication Data

Feldmann, Doug.
Curriculum and the American rural school / Doug Feldmann.
p.   cm.
l. Education, Rural—United States—Curricula. 2. Curriculum
change—United States—History. I. Title.

LC5146.5.F45 2003   375'.0009173'4—dc21   2003048432 CIP

ISBN 0-7618-2558-4 (paperback : alk. ppr.)

⊖™ The paper used in this publication meets the minimum
requirements of American National Standard for Information
Sciences—Permanence of Paper for Printed Library Materials,
ANSI Z39.48—1984

To educators in all communities – particularly those in rural areas – who strive to build a promising future for our nation.

Contents

Preface

The far-reaching images that are emblazoned on our minds are truly amazing. The smell of a cigar can take us back to the childhood memory of a baseball park or a barber shop; a song on the radio can take us back to the young-adult memory of a loved one or a conversion experience. For our lives are indeed measured in increments of time – clear, distinct epochs into which we categorize the most cherished and despised moments of our lives. And a whiff of a cigar or a single note from a song can jar those memories into consciousness.

Moreover, this consciousness is at once both individual and collective; for while every person has that secret "special place" that only he or she knows about (and *is* special for reasons known only to the individual), there are artifacts from our communal living that bind us together into groups. The most obvious of these are the items that comprise our "communities," whereby we form cohesive bonds with people in our immediate area. Physical entities such as the church, the school, the grocery store, and the office of the local insurance agent are landmarks for our past, each a brush stroke on the complex portraits of our lives. Even so it is imagined, in this age of technology, that we are now creating *communities without place* – for one can now e-mail a favorite poem to a friend in California, take a college course from a school in Oregon, or watch a football game from Alabama through the satellite dish – all from the comforts of home in Connecticut, or wherever else.

Are we, then, losing the sense of community in its originally-intended form? Or did the original form of community become too invasive in our modern, private world, in which we are doing more and more of our Christmas shopping online?

Part of what community represents is the honored local culture that is transmitted to its young people; in a formal sense, this takes shape in the curriculum of the local school. Over history, and for reasons sometimes known only to the "change agent," educators have attempted to change what children learn in various communities. Some of these efforts were successful and others not, and some of the changes occurred within the community and others originated from outside its boundaries. It seems true that change does indeed come slower to certain areas of our society. When change is sought, care must be taken that the recipients of the change are in favor of it, let alone being allowed to participate in the process of the change.

Part of the purpose of this book, therefore, is to examine not only how curriculum affects the transmission of culture in American rural schools, but also how the vectors of the "change winds" can stir emotions of defensiveness or aggressiveness in a given community. It has been humored in educational circles that, when Rip Van Winkle finally awoke, the most comforting place for him to have gone would have been the local school – for unlike other things, little had changed in the school from the time he fell asleep. However, as educators, lawmakers, or simply concerned citizens, we must always be careful to consider all the ramifications of the changes we seek to make in schooling. Newer isn't always better, and "change for change's sake" isn't always a good idea. Let us temper our open-mindedness to new ideas with a willful preservation of what's already good.

Doug Feldmann

Introduction

"What is school for?"

This question has been asked for centuries, in various ways, by students, teachers, taxpayers, historians, bureaucrats, and nearly everyone else. It is no less prominent today than when Plato detailed the famous conversation in ancient times between Socrates and Meno on the subject. For when one sifts through all of the political footballing of public education that occurs in the twenty-first century United States, this question is the inevitable ending point to discussion and debate on educational processes. Sub-questions that typically follow include: Is it the role of the public and private schools of America to produce good citizens through an inundation of civic training? Is it the role of schools to impart knowledge through rigorous training in time-honored subjects, such as the humanities? Is it the role of the schools to transmit the cultural heritage? Or, is it the schools' role to allow for the development of the child in ways that are relatively untested, yet apparently natural to children's interests and desires?

At the heart of any of these questions (among others) is the presence of the school *curriculum* – an entity that was not conceived in the United States, in a broad sense, until the end of the 1800s. The rapidly-changing American society in the late nineteenth century prompted policymakers to shift control of what was being taught in classrooms from working teachers to comprehensive documents. No longer should individual teachers hold the control, it was decided, but rather an inanimate, centralized, core body of knowledge. With a curricular frenzy commencing in the United States at this point, the country soon discovered that lying behind the *purpose of schooling* that any nation, state, or municipality has embraced is the concept of a curriculum that serves as the academic guiding force.

The curriculum has been masked by the terms "standards," "performance-based objectives," and other nomenclature. But for all its cosmetic changes over four hundred years, the concept of schooling on American shores remains the same: a place where children are expected to build their schema by processing new and more challenging material as they progress through the system. Whether teachers can find the piece of paper that "says so" or not, they are all guided by that container of expectations known as the curriculum.

With the birth of curriculum use in American schools (generally accepted as beginning with the recommendations of the Committee of Ten in 1893), it is understandable that the guardians of traditional subject matter assumed the first control. Not soon after, however, a number of groups – initially calling themselves "child-centered," "social efficiency educators," and other things, but eventually all calling themselves "progressives" (perhaps mistakenly) – burst onto the scene to join the unstable situation of the American "curriculum debate." From the mid-1890s through the 1920s, several camps came forward with what they felt were the best blueprints for the course education should take in the United States. As in a heavyweight boxing match with two power punchers, the traditional group pitted itself against the newcomers (as an entire group) and exchanged punishing blows, but none left the melee clearly the victor. As Kliebard (1995a) noted when the smoke cleared, "No single interest group ever gained absolute supremacy... In the end, what became the American curriculum was not the result of any decisive victory by any of the contending parties, but a loose, largely unarticulated, and not very tidy compromise" (p. 25)

One catalyst of this curricular debate was the mass urbanization of the United States in the late 1800s and early 1900s. For reasons as plentiful as the individuals themselves, people flocked to the cities – particularly in the North – to escape rural hardships resulting from land no longer being arable, mines no longer being productive, and deserted remote areas with no more consumers with spending money. It seemed that the American city, strong and imposing, held the key to riches for a better life. Those witnessing the great migration firsthand even had difficulty explaining the phenomenon, such as George Betts (1913). "The causes lying back of the rapid growth of our cities at the expense of our rural districts are very far from simple. They involve a great complex of social, educational, and economic forces" (p. ix). For many, there was indeed an improved way of life to be found in the city; and, as tax bases took hold, the establishment of solid public schools did so as well. Money soon came in short supply to the country schools, however. "In more than one respect, the rural school has not participated in the fruits of our educational progress," noted Stanford University professor Ellwood Cubberly in 1912 (p. vi). He continued by describing the bursting city craze as "pathological." "The modern industrial city, with its peculiar pathological conditions, has commanded both public and professional interest, but the rural community and the rural school have been neglected..." (pp. v-vii).

As the cities continued to grow and prosper, a considerable contingent stayed behind in the American small town. In the initial stages of this emigration, government officials and educational policymakers appeared to show concern for these people; if society continued to change at this rapid pace, will not these rural citizens be left even further behind? It was mandated, therefore, that policymakers would prepare rural people for what life was to be like in the twentieth century – a lifestyle to be dominated by the urban scene. It was decided that the little "one-room schoolhouses" that provided instruction for children in agrarian sectors must ready their students for this type of society. It was noticed by only a relative few that rural areas were being left in the wake of this change.

Thus began the history of educational policy in the United States in making a "force-fitting" of unilateral doctrines on all rural schools. Ideas constructed by educators and legislators at the national and state levels were mistakenly seen as applicable to every agrarian system, whereas many local districts interpreted the policies in various ways. To achieve some sort of commonality, even policymakers developed lists of competencies that rural students must attain.

Since that point, curriculum has taken a substantially different course in rural schools than its urban and suburban counterparts. The development of curriculum in rural schools was altered the most by one single, sweeping policy (some claim adversely, others positively) – the waves of school consolidation movements that washed through the countryside. The consolidation of smaller school systems into larger ones was thought to benefit students by providing greater curricular opportunities, along with (presumably) better instruction occurring as well. Not considered, however, were the unseen ramifications of consolidating: the arduous travel for students, the loss of personal identity for individual towns, and the cultural clashes between communities that soon followed. As with many other American educational policies illustrated by Kliebard (1995a), the practice of consolidation reared its head for a while, went below the surface, and then rose again several times over. Its greatest push would occur in the late 1950s, as James Conant produced his influential reports on American secondary education based on what he perceived as the inadequacies of small schools.

Over the ages, Americans have appeared to agreed upon one incontrovertible fact: that the most assured way to reform society, however long it might take, is through the reformation of the public education system. Quite often, these reforms have been important to only the reformers themselves, and few others; it is arguable that pure, true, systemic change has never occurred in American public education (at least in a revolutionary sense, for many movements have certainly evolved over time). Nevertheless, attempts at quick changes to the system were made, and continue to be made. Ventures with charter schools, home schooling, school choice, alternative schools, and many other concepts have been forged. Unfortunately, in most cases, money runs out to support these programs in the long run, as finite grant funding causes a terminal atmosphere for an effort before it even begins. What runs out more often, however, is patience. While reform of the public education system may indeed be the truest avenue of societal reform, it is also the slowest. In the twenty-first century, slow response is not tolerated, be it while waiting for an auto repair or access to an Internet site. In our generation we do not have time to wait, regardless of the project and its scope. In a like manner, it is impatience that causes the doom of school-related reform. The principles of American pedagogy are so deeply embedded that a 180-degree shift in its operation may well never occur.

At certain points, some reform movements have nonetheless "shook the pillars" of the establishment. Allowing families more choice in where their children will attend school has taken root in some places, while the number of charters issued by various states for special-interest schools has grown as well. Still at the heart of any reform movement, however, is the debate over *what should be taught in school*, what children should know, or what they should be able to do – once again, returning attention to the term "curriculum."

As the American curricular debate widened into the 1900s, some curricular changes that were rooted in urban districts impacted the rural educational scene as well. The most notable among these in the early part of the century was the Cardinal Principles of Secondary Education, issued in 1918 by a National Education Association posse led by Brooklyn math teacher Clarence Kingsley. More than any other, this document shifted the focus of instruction in American schools from the traditional content areas to the honing of personal traits, such as civic and domestic duties. While maintaining local cultures and customs within their communities and schools, rural areas tended to follow suit, as rural school superintendents arrived back in their hometowns with new suggestions from the big-city educators. In the early part of the twentieth century, the NEA was not the lobbying union as it is known today; rather, it served more as a forum for sharing research, or a yearly gathering for the discussion of educational trends across the country (as is carried out today by groups such as the American Educational Research Association). Few practicing teachers, however, attended the NEA conventions; the majority of the participants were college faculty and school superintendents.

In modern times, it has been technology that has drastically altered the course of rural school curriculum. The notion of "distance learning" – or the transmission of live-taught classroom instruction to another location – was initially seen as a panacea for rural schools with limited curricula. As with consolidation, however, it was the "unseen" aspects of distance learning that slowed its effectual spread through the educational domain. Some teachers found it unnerving to teach in front of a television camera, to coordinate two locations of human beings at once, or simply relying on the technology to be functional (or *functioning*) for each and every class meeting. So once again (as with consolidation and, as will be seen later, the Committee of Ten's and the Committee of Twelve's recommendations), what was seen as a universal "magic bullet" for rural school problems –

particularly those dealing with curriculum – became wrought with localized problems.

History has proven that a single recommendation or policy is not a universal fit for all rural areas and schools. Within each school (and particularly, schools in rural communities), even though a formal curriculum (school board-approved and administratively-circulated) often exists, the term "curriculum" can be vague and include much more than the identifiable document. It may include the instructional processes of individual classrooms, the assessment procedures of individual classrooms, the unspoken desires of the community, or a multitude of other factors that contribute to the actual teaching and learning journey that takes place within the school. As Clandinin and Connelly (1992) noted, curriculum has a "tangled definitional history" (p. 364). They suggest they "recently attempted what we like to think of as a Deweyan view of curriculum from a teacher's vantage point. John Dewey's (1938) notion of 'situation' and 'experience' enabled us to imagine the teacher not so much as a maker of curriculum but as a part of it… " (p. 365). In other words, it may be possible to view curriculum outside of being a document, and part of the socialization of a teacher into his or her working environment. And, with cultures and values differing from one rural town to the next, the issue becomes even more complex.

Kliebard (1975) also acknowledges the troubling task of defining curriculum.

> This problem involves a clarification of the chaotic state of curriculum terminology, a problem alluded to by many leaders in the curriculum field since the 1920s. A variety of widely differing programs, for example, have been proposed and implemented under the names of the activity curriculum or the experience curriculum. (p. 43)

Therefore, with confusion surrounding the use of the term "curriculum," it will be defined in the following manner for use in this book. It is possible to look at curriculum in two ways: that which is a *field of study* and that which is a *document*. The field has been filled with over eighty years of theories, theoreticians, philosophical camps, policy debates, and research methodology. Many educational scholars point to Franklin Bobbitt's 1918 book, *The Curriculum,* as the origin of curriculum as a bona fide field of study (Longstreet & Shane, 1993; Kliebard, 1995a). Along with commencing the discipline, Bobbitt and his contemporaries simultaneously made the case for what was to become known as "scientific curriculum-making" as they attempted to conduct a careful, systematic study of society and its needs as the basis for choosing objectives in the curriculum. As Beyer and Liston (1996) note, "For men like Franklin Bobbitt (1918), W.W. Charters (1923), David Snedden (1921), and Ross Finney (1928) – virtually the 'founding fathers' of the curriculum field – the school was to be modeled after the factory" (p. 19). This emerging field of educational theory, it was imagined, would help establish a new plan for the operation of schools and would eliminate waste; the differing interests and abilities of teachers would give way to a unified plan of instruction. For, until that point, the teacher was considered the focus and main source of content matter in the American classroom (Kaestle, 1983).

Since Bobbitt's work, the theory produced by the field (in its almost infinite varieties) has attempted to answer the question posed by the nineteenth-century English philosopher Herbert Spencer, "What knowledge is of most worth?" Many theories in education have been likened to a pendulum, shifting back and forth over time. However, as will be illustrated in the early chapters of this book, different theoretical positions rose over the course of the twentieth century that were more "streamlike" than pendulumatic, surfacing when the conditions were right, as Kliebard (1995a) puts it, and then going below the surface when social conditions did not warrant their presence.

Within the field of curriculum, however, theories and philosophies have varied greatly. Bobbitt's idea of scientific curriculum-making met with initial resistance, such as from the early reconstructionists Harold Rugg and George Counts, who sought to free the student from the factory-like constraints of the behaviorist mode of study (Kliebard, 1995a). Put another way, a debate was ignited in the field between a "subject-centered" and "child-centered" approach to curriculum. This debate continues today. In the contemporary framework of the field, conservative views may suggest more of a "back-to-basics," subject-centered approach (see Bloom, 1987; Hirsch, 1987). On the contrary, a more liberal stance may endorse a curriculum that is centered within the interests of the child (see Apple, 1975; Giroux, 1983). With the uncertainty that yet pervades the term "curriculum" today, this debate is likely to continue into the next century.

As Rugg (1938) once stated, "There is no more crucial job in the entire gamut of community life than that of the curriculum designer" (p. 8). The curriculum of a school is often considered to be at the heart of a particular community's values; in other words, residents and school personnel, naturally, are often careful in pondering what should be taught to their children. Ornstein and Hunkins (1988) believe that a philosophical base is the pre-requisite to any type of curriculum-making. "It becomes evident that many aspects of curriculum, if not most of the educational process in school, are developed around philosophy... curriculum workers need to provide assistance in developing and designing school practices that coincide with the philosophy of the school and community" (pp. 55-58).

This idea is most noticeable in a rural, small-town school system, in which the close proximity (and small numbers) of residents may provide for a more unified consensus regarding curricular content. Kilpatrick (1936) noted that small communities provided for a more wholesome educational experience than what was, at the time, being developed in the larger American cities – particularly in regard to *what was being taught* in the schools. This suggests it is important to understand the nature of curricular dialogue, and how the particular environment leads to the end product of a formal curriculum. An exploration of the intimate nature of a rural high school faculty, therefore, may often uncover unique processes and products in regard to curricular formation; this phenomenon will be examined ethnographically later in this book.

In attempting to keep up with this theory being produced (and consequently changed) by academicians and policymakers, individual school systems across the United States have produced curricular *documents* over the past century trying to reflect what educrats currently term as "best practice." However, when translated through the national-state-community-school-classroom chain, curriculum's version of the "phone game" – what children play when whispering the same phrase to each other, with the final version completely different from the beginning one – proved what a truly local item it inevitably was. What began as a presumably infallible curricular theory in some college of education on the East Coast became something totally different in Mrs. Johnson's third grade classroom in Bartelso, Illinois.

Therefore, in light of this view, there may actually be two curricula at work simultaneously within the "document" area – the "formal" curriculum and the "enacted" curriculum. In this definition, the *formal* curriculum is the paper approved by the school board or other governing body, sitting as the "official answer" to content issues and discrepancies within the school system. At a given high school, for example, the "formal" curriculum may be inactive, though present; it may consist of scattered documents that lurk, untouched for years, in the filing cabinets behind the desk of the principal. As inactive as that "filed" curriculum may seem, therefore, one could argue that a formal curriculum does not exist. Naturally, the teachers may be unaware of any formal curriculum to guide their instruction. On the contrary, the *enacted* curriculum refers to how knowledge is transferred from teacher to student – the existence of a formal written curriculum notwithstanding. For when the classroom teacher shuts her door to begin the school day – be it in a rural, urban, or suburban school – the components of the formal curriculum are enacted in a way that suits the interests, abilities, and professional choices of that teacher.

The differences between the formal and enacted curriculum are described another way by Pratt (1980), who suggests that a curriculum is not a system of activities, but a "blueprint" or "plan." The plan itself may exist on paper (the formal curriculum) but yet needs to have its parts integrated into the whole of the school. From this point, it is translated into organized intentions for the learners in individual classrooms (the enacted curriculum).

But, for America's rural schools, perhaps the most powerful aspect is not in the curriculum field or the curriculum document, but rather in what some have called the *hidden curriculum*. In most schools, it is generally accepted that reading, writing, arithmetic, and other selected subjects are to be studied. However, what the "other subjects" are and how they and the core subjects are taught can be quite different. After-school activities deemed "appropriate" by certain communities may differ as well, and this is also part of the hidden curriculum. The hidden curriculum can also affect non-instructional actions in the school, such as the candidate-selection processes when teacher and administrator vacancies are posted. This was illustrated in Alan Peshkin's (1978) celebrated ethnography of

"Mansfield" Ohio, where such considerations assumed great importance in hiring practices. In choosing a new superintendent, the Mansfield school board ultimately found the qualification they had to have, by unspoken mandate of the community.

> ...After hearing their deliberations, who could doubt that they sought a person who would administer the school system in their spirit, true to the prevailing outlook? "He's country," they agreed, and thereby reassured themselves. (p. 82)

With the idea of the hidden curriculum, the term curriculum refers to the "operational code" for the community. The hidden curriculum will not be found anywhere on paper, but is circulates throughout the air of the town – it is part of each and every activity of the school. Strictly speaking, the values and mores of the community shine through. Therefore, with the impact of the hidden curriculum, following the formal curriculum to the letter of the law is a painstaking (and most likely, impossible) task for the rural school teacher.

Perhaps an even more challenging situation is when teachers in a rural school system undertake the process of "making" curriculum. The very nature of curriculum involves an interpretive component on the part of each teacher; thus, the process of a school staff developing a formal curriculum can be inherently problematic. Furthermore, Pinar (1995) even suggests that "the era of curriculum development is past" (p. 5); that in the modern, multi-definitional age of curriculum, it is impossible to converge all necessary discourses and theories into a comprehensive curricular product. Further evidence exists that obsolete texts serve as the curriculum of the day, nullifying the need for development – and that "these out-of-date but still-in-print books silence the voices of many important, but sometimes younger, intellectually more complex scholars..." (Ibid.). Thus, it is argued that a truly thorough curriculum – accurate with all the necessary voices – is beyond the capability of construction in contemporary times. And as Beyer and Liston (1996) noted, "When it comes to the practice of schooling, the community and institutional contexts, the national educational mood, and past curricular practices, all affect what can and will be viewed as defensible curricular offerings and practices" (p. 199). Hirsch (1996) even asserts that the idea of an American school curriculum is a "myth"; he challenges any citizen to "simply ask the principal of your nearest elementary school for a description of the minimal specific content that all children at a grade level are supposed to learn. Those who have tried this experiment have come away empty-handed" (p. 27). So then, what is a small-town, rural educator to do when faced with the task of providing a curricular roadmap for the students that he or she serves?

As difficult as understanding the profound concept of curriculum may be, the task of constructing it is even larger. When faced with this duty, the teacher in the modern American rural school is forced to juggle a variety of concerns: the maintenance of local customs, the inclusion of modern technology and learning theory, limited physical and financial resources, and quite often, a transitive administration that uses the smaller school system as a "stepping stone" to a more lucrative principalship or superintendency. Although many school administrators in rural areas are truly committed to their communities, a large percentage do leave their positions after only a short time (see Boone, 1998).

Furthermore, on top of dwindling tax bases and structural resources, rural areas of the country continue to be undermined and underestimated. According to the United States Census Bureau, approximately 1.2 percent of all rural residents were missed in the 1990 census – along with 5.9 percent of rural citizens who rent their property, as compared with 4.2 percent of urban renters (USDC, 1999). And while rural schools represented 22 percent of all public schools in the United States in 1997, they received only 12.5 percent of all federal funding, 14 percent of all state funding, and 11 percent of all local funding (U.S. Department of Education, 2000). The problems of urban America are well-documented, well-publicized, and certainly important, but it is the plight of rural sectors of the country that mostly go unrecognized and unaided. Meanwhile, however, these same rural areas are expected to produce young people from its school systems that will be productive members of the urbanized society – as was the case after the Committee of Twelve issued its recommendations in 1897, to be seen later in this book.

So again, the question: "What is school for?" Kliebard (1975) proposes that "the broad question of what education is for or what is a good education is one that pervades all of the field of education and is not particularly distinctive to the curriculum field"

(p. 45).   To be certain, the process of schooling transcends the curriculum and ventures out into the areas of teacher and administrator quality, community support, financial resources, and a host of other factors.   In light of many hindrances and issues, in particular those of curriculum, this question is perhaps most complex – and most important to be answered – in the rural sectors of our nation.

1. Development of the American Curriculum and the Rural Response

It is hard for an empty sack to stand upright.

– Benjamin Franklin

In colonial America, there was little "code" to guide education. With the dominance of religion, civil law had little bearing on the lives of citizens; the law of God was what mattered, and people were expected to follow it. In a like manner, there was not a set curriculum to follow for the few organized schools that existed, outside of the sectarian expectations of New England. Much of the formal education was reserved for boys preparing for ministry.

Even the staunch Puritans, however, began to see value in a codification of school training for their young people. Thus, one could argue that curriculum in the United States began with the Old Satan Deluder Act established by the Puritans in 1647. It was perhaps more "educational legislation" than curriculum, but was nonetheless the first attempt at some type of instructional organization on New World shores by the Europeans. With training supplemented by approved texts, the Puritans sought to have their children avoid evil by keeping them busy with noble pursuits. "Being the chiefe project of that ould deluder, Satan," it claimed, "to keepe men from the knowledge of the scriptures" (Urban and Waggoner, 1996, p. 37). The act stated that towns with fifty or more families must furnish a reading and writing teacher. If the town grew to one hundred or more families, it needed to provide a teacher of Latin to prepare boys for seminary training at Harvard (which was founded in 1636). Whether the Puritans were aware of it or not, they launched the stormy debate of curriculum selection that has raged in America for nearly four centuries.

The *New England Primer*, which served as one of the main textbooks in Puritan education, was still being widely circulated into the 1700s. It contained moral lessons as well linguistic ones, as pupils learned rhymes such as "In Adam's fall, we sinned all." There was strict adherence to the Puritan values in the majority of the educational sphere; so much so, in fact, that in 1701 a group of disgruntled Congregationalists broke away from Harvard and founded Yale University, claiming that the Harvards had become to religiously tolerant in their admission and instructional practices. Princeton University entered the fray in 1746, as it was chartered by Presbyterians who also wanted to train their own ministers. The opening of Princeton coincided with a push during the mid-1700s known as the "Great Awakening," a turn from the doom-laden creed of the Puritans and to one of more hopefulness.

Ultimately, however, as the cultural pluralism of the nation became more apparent with the unification of New England with the middle and southern colonies, a new school textbook called *The McGuffey Reader* came on the scene to take the *Primer's* place. As political tensions rose with the motherland of England, *McGuffey* would be used to teach lessons to students that had more of a patriotic tone than the *Primer*. And even after the United States had won her independence from Great Britain, the book would continue as a centerpiece of American education as far along as early part of the 1900s.

Among his other laurels, Benjamin Franklin was perhaps also the first widely-recognized American philosopher on the subjects of education and curriculum. His utilitarian message was made famous by his claim that "much of the knowledge in use is not of much use." He also may have been the first to suggest breaking colonial school instruction away from the traditional subjects – primarily Latin, Greek, and History – into more of a pragmatic mode.

To this end, he sponsored the establishment of "academies" where the time-honored subjects would be available (and still encouraged) but not required. To ensure a breadth of study, Franklin furthered his famous phrase above by continuing "... it would be well if they [students] could be taught everything that is useful, and everything that is ornamental; but art is long, and their time is short. It is therefore proposed that they learn those things that are likely to be most useful and most ornamental" (Willis, et al., 1994, pp. 17-18).

While America was taking off as a growing nation into the 1800s, a new spirit of academic adventure was engulfing the world. This new era, called "The Age of Enlightenment," had brought exciting new discoveries in the sciences; and it was believed by some that the long-held mysteries of the universe were finally being revealed to human beings. This excitement, however, did not quite propel the United States into her great experiment in public education just yet; that leap would come later in the century. Formal education in the early nineteenth century was still reserved for the privileged classes, as most of the higher education institutions were still training boys for leadership or clerical roles, and the traditional nature of their curricula did not mesh well with the new-found discoveries in the sciences. There appeared to be no room in the traditional course of study for the new sciences, as language, history, rhetoric, mathematics, and geography continued to dominate, and the newly-devised "elective" system was given little credibility by most in the college ranks. To reinforce this point, the Yale faculty issued a report in 1828 reaffirming the traditional curriculum against what they called the "intrusion" of modern subjects, particularly in the sciences. The report, headed by Yale President Jeremiah Day and Professor James Kingsley, sought to head off the invasion before it could take root in upper-level instruction. The mavericks that were attempting to inculcate modern science – known as the Deists – promoted the view that the discovery of contemporary inquiry had been a "gift from God," allowing human beings to finally unravel the secrets of the ages. The rebels could not overcome the academic establishment, however, and the traditional subject matter supported in the Yale Faculty Report would dominate American curriculum for the next seventy years – and yet today, some would argue.

Horace Mann and the Common School Movement

Even though the traditional subject matter had been endorsed by the most powerful voices in the land, the curriculum was not widely executed by the 1840s, for those receiving this instruction continued to be a relative few. This seemed incredulous to a young Massachusetts politician named Horace Mann, who took up a crusade for what he called a "common education" for all free citizens. A lawyer by training, he had graduated from Brown University in 1819 and developed a law practice in Boston before heading to the legislature. When he lost his wife to an illness, he became somewhat disenchanted with politics and sought a mission in life that would have greater meaning beyond his own living days. It was Mann himself that cast the deciding vote in the creation of Massachusetts' first state board of education in 1837, and he was immediately named its first secretary – a post he would hold for eleven years, when in 1848 he filled the Massachusetts Senate seat left vacant by the death of John Quincy Adams. Mann dreamed of a proliferated educational system that would become "the Great Equalizer of society... the balance wheel of the social machinery." Mann looked to common schools as the ultimate source of moral education for students, and much of his philosophy was drawn from the writings of President Andrew Jackson, who presided in the Oval Office from 1828 to 1836. Jackson, from Tennessee, was known as the "Champion of Common Men" and was the first President born outside of Virginia or Massachusetts. Jackson's appeal to the common man stemmed from his status as a military hero (for disbanding hostile Indian tribes in 1812) and for breaking up the monopoly of the federal American bank.

Mann's plea for the establishment of such a common school system initially fell on deaf ears, however – particularly in the circles of the business class. The idea of an educated laborer did not appeal to business leaders, as they imagined their employees demanding greater pay or even ownership in the business as they became better educated. Mann, however, was able to convince them of quite an opposite scenario. He contended that an educated worker was more likely to show up on time, show up sober, save money, and best of all – work more productively and efficiently. At the root of social depravity, Mann believed, was the growing disparity of wealth in the United States. "Poverty is a public as well as a private evil," he said. "The earth contains abundant resources for ten times – doubtless for twenty times – its present inhabitants... millions are perishing in the midst of superfluities" (1848, p. 120). He decried the ceaseless investment in industry, railroads, and business, all appearing to profit only a select few. "The greatest of all the arts in the political economy is to change a consumer into a producer," he continued. "And the next greatest is to increase the producer's producing power – an end to be directly attained by increasing his intelligence" (ibid., p. 131).

With the support of other politicians and the bourgeoisie finally with him, Mann's efforts led to the nation's first compulsory attendance law for schools, which appeared in Massachusetts in 1852. Two years later, Mann would leave Massachusetts to assume his final role in professional life, becoming the president of Antioch College in Ohio.

Mann was also aided by the efforts of Henry Barnard of Connecticut, who had sowed the roots of common education in that state as early as 1838. Barnard, like Mann, was a politician by trade, and had been elected by the Whig Party to the Connecticut legislature in 1837. Within a year, he was encouraged with the inroads made by Mann in Massachusetts and pushed the Connecticut assembly for the establishment of its own common school system. His effort in this area was relatively short-lived, however, as his call for higher taxes to support the school system angered his constituents, and he was removed from the legislature in 1842. After a stint in furthering the common school movement in Rhode Island, he returned to Connecticut in 1851 to resume the cause in his home state.

Barnard was also behind the push for expanding the normal school concept for training educators, as he noted, "employing a teacher with only so much knowledge as he is required to communicate... is a serious practical evil" (Willis, et al., 1994, p. 41). To this time – and throughout the remainder of the 1800s – little attention was paid to the qualifications of teachers. A few basic qualities were sought, however, as noted by David Page (1849), Principal of the State Normal School of Albany, New York.

> "Neatness... this implies cleanliness of the person. If some who assume to teach were not proverbial for their slovenliness, I would not dwell on this point... order... it is of great moment to the teacher, that, when he demands order and arrangement among his pupils, they cannot

> appeal to any breach of it in his own practice... courtesy...
> all vulgar jesting should forever be excluded from his
> mouth... I cannot find words to express my astonishment at
> the indifference of parents, or at the recklessness of
> teachers, wherever I know such cases to exist. (pp. 40-41)

As the early returns came in, it looked as if Mann's efforts would be an immediate success. The dollar value of school textbooks produced in the United States tripled between 1840 and 1860. Unfortunately, however, the compulsory attendance law was difficult to enforce. By 1890, 27 states would have such laws; by 1918, all 48 did. These statutes were certainly measures of good faith by the state governments, and as Cubberly (1912) noted, "The boy or girl most worth paying for is the one who wants to go to school for the longest time" (p. 24). Nonetheless, forcing a blue-collar family's children to attend school rather than having them work and help bolster the family income was indeed a hard sell. Despite the laws, state governments were admittedly not in the business of visiting schools and checking attendance records, particularly in outlying rural areas. In 1790, 95% of the U.S. population lived in communities of 2,500 or fewer residents; by 1830, however the figure had slipped only slightly to 91%. Any type of common education that existed within rural communities to this time was heavily controlled by the local parents, including the selection of textbooks, selection of the teacher, and the length of the school year.

Due to low pay, poor working conditions, and very little respect from the general public, qualified and willing teachers for rural schools were in short supply. Formal education was so maligned in rural areas in the nineteenth century, in fact, that common textbooks were not even readily available for students sharing the same classroom. When a rural community did decide to create a communal gathering place in which children would receive instruction, such schools were usually built on abandoned farmland which was no longer good for growing crops. These places, often dubbed as "field schools," epitomized the low public sentiment towards the classroom.

In the most impoverished areas, the books used in the one-room schoolhouses usually consisted of what students were able to bring from home. In some cases, that meant only a Bible; in others, it meant an occasional newspaper or perhaps nothing at all. With this lack of uniformity in resources, the curriculum of the American rural school in the 1800s frequently became a mirror reflection of the teacher in charge. The pupils were at the academic mercy of the teacher, jotting down the tidbits of information that the instructor was able to provide (and often, the students were at the *physical* mercy of the teacher also, as corporal punishment – even for the most minute offenses – was the order of the day). The individuals that were teaching in the rural schools in the Nineteenth Century, unfortunately, "were often portrayed as drunken, foreign, and ignorant," according to Kaestle (1983, p. 20). It was seen that comprehensive, systemic action was needed to address this shortage if public education in the United States would eventually thrive.

Teacher Training and the Advent of Normal Schools

The formalization of teacher training saw its roots take hold in 1839, when Barnard and Emma Willard opened their "Teachers Institute" in Connecticut. In actuality, the training was not extensive; often, the sessions lasted for only a few weeks. The candidates were given basic practice in lesson theory and application, and the idea of producing a "common teacher" soon spread across many parts of the country. The focus of the training evolved to become an evaluation of the moral character of the candidates; the sessions were used to identify and fortify the moral grounding of the potential teachers, and to make sure that this moral grounding was passed along to the teachers' future students. And, with the enrollees at these institutes primarily being women in the nineteenth century, it was clear that society viewed the female as needing more stringent moral training for classroom work than their male counterparts.

As noted by Spring (1986), the idea of normal school training in the United States was taken from Prussian culture. When normal schools grew in number and structure in the late 1800s, they began to assume a very specific role in American education. Whereas teachers being trained for the newly-formed secondary common schools arrived from colleges and universities, those serving in elementary schools were the products of the new normal institutions. This was furthered by the decision of Michigan Supreme Court Justice Thomas M. Cooley, who in 1872 affirmed the right of local school board to levy taxes to support secondary education; soon after, the first tax-supported high school in the United States opened in Kalamazoo. So while the availability of teachers was beginning to improve, greater sources of income were still being sought.

The idea of a widespread, multi-level, tax-supported public school system in the United States was still a ways off in 1853 when a brash, young North Carolina politician named Calvin Wiley stepped to the forefront. The common school movement had already swept down from the Northeast, more residue from the work of Mann in Massachusetts. An 1839 law in North Carolina had given local areas the power to decide on the need for formal schools in their locales, as well as the decision whether to levy taxes for the support of such a cause. What Wiley suggested in his first year as State Superintendent of Common Schools in 1853, however, was truly unique: to augment the number and quality of teachers for North Carolina schools by establishing local "training centers" for teachers, and to have individual counties oversee an examination and certification process for the teachers who served in their schools. Within seven years, it was obvious that Wiley's plan was a success: over 90 percent of the state's teachers had achieved official licensure, and consequently commanded salaries that were comparable with the wealthier states of the North.

With North Carolina as a leader in the education of teachers, other states in the rural South began to follow suit. Thus, as education gradually became viewed as a "profession" – for both teacher and student – citizens in states previously averse to formal schooling began discovering the benefits. However, the American Civil War brought a quick end to this momentum, and with reconstruction continuing through the late 1870s, most southern states returned to a disdain for spending public tax revenue on organized education. This was tempered to a certain degree, however, with the establishment of educational grants for the South by George Peabody, a wealthy financier, in 1869 at a total of $2 million. The grants soon became endowed, and were a source of impetus for educational change throughout the former Confederacy (Rippa, 1992). The work of Peabody led to the founding of the Peabody College for Teachers in Nashville, Tennessee, which was chartered in 1909. This provided for a sort of Gibraltar of teacher education in the region, a centralizing force that would contribute to both the campaign for and production of quality teachers for rural areas in that part of the country.

Whether it was in the North or South, however, the presence of a qualified teacher in a rural school was at times lessened by the agricultural trends of a given community. Seasonal restrictions in rural areas (and the consequent adherence to the agrarian calendar) also reinforced patterns of teacher employment in the local schools. Rural schools typically carried two sessions – winter and summer – with attendance based on need in the fields. With male labor required in the summer months, the attendance of boys was scant; so was the presence of a male teacher. Conversely, females were noticeably absent in the classroom during the winter months as the boys returned to take their places at the desks. The history of the schools in rural Clark County, Illinois between 1862 and 1879 noted by Pinar (1995) highlighted a microcosm of the operational patterns of rural schools during this era.

> During this seventeen year period there were two terms each year [winter and summer], with thirty-four teacher contracts signed. Of these thirty-four, twenty were signed by men, fourteen by women (in contrast to urban schools were women teachers constituted a majority). All fourteen women teachers taught summer terms. Salary equity for men and women teachers would wait until the twentieth century. Over the seventeen-year period, the average monthly salary for male teachers was $33; for female teachers, $17. (p. 85)

Due to factors such as this, it was the rural areas of the country that had the most difficult time in securing quality teachers. And while the idea of the need for manual labor in the fields seems to be one of the past, this issue is present yet today – masked by the assumed takeover of modern machinery.

As the second half of the nineteenth century took shape, the Yale Faculty Report continued its dominion over what was taught in colleges and universities. Few dared to stray from the traditional curriculum, although cracks in the wall were beginning to form. When Cornell and Johns Hopkins were founded in 1868 and 1876 respectively, each was primarily devoted to graduate study only. However, for the first time, widespread research was beginning to occur outside of the liberal arts. While private colleges were still the norm in the eastern part of the United States, public land-grant universities were beginning to form across the Midwest.

The disparity in wealth between urban and rural schools was relatively unseen in the middle part of the nineteenth century. The larger cities in the U.S. were not quite large at all to that point, and thus no significant tax base existed to public fund a superior educational system. The gulf between city and farm quickly widened, however, as people began flocking to the cities in great numbers. Countless industries were established, and with it the procurement of taxable income – part of the human resources of which was taken from rural areas. Furthermore, as private and parochial schools continued to develop in urban areas and vanish in rural ones, a taxpayer became available to city schools whose children were not taking the benefits of the public system.

The lack of coherence in textbooks and teacher quality, along with a wide variance in attendance patterns of farm students, provided for an inconsistent and highly localized rural curriculum that was forming in the United States in the 1800s. Toward the end of the century, educators on the national scene would begin to attempt to shape what was conceived to be a singular "rural curriculum," one that was presumed to serve all rural areas in their scholastic needs for the emerging twentieth century. But with the explosion of schools on the American scene, many were even beginning to see the need for a "national" curriculum, a common guide for all schools to follow in their instruction.

2. A National Curriculum: William Torrey Harris and the Committee of Ten, 1893

> Our schools have been scientifically designed to prevent over-education from happening.
>
> – William Torrey Harris

By the 1870s the city of St. Louis, like other urban areas around the country at the time, was finally experiencing foreseeable problems with the development of a public school system for its children. A bustling industrial core was beginning to form, and a stream of post-Civil War workseekers hit the city along with their families. Providing enough jobs for the wage earners was not a problem; providing a quality education for their children was. To remedy the situation, the St. Louis Board of Education brought in a deep-thinking philosopher from the East. His name was William Torrey Harris, and he sought to provide an efficient, thorough, public-school education for all of the city's children.

As soon as Harris arrived on the job in 1869, he constructed a graded, quarterly program for the city schools – the original model of the graded system known today. Harris believed that the graded program would ensure smooth transfer of students from one level of study to the next. Wishing to trim down any unnecessary waste, he pored over volumes of statistics on the school system's expenditures, teacher characteristics, student attendance, and academic profiles from previous years. Already a national figure in philosophy at age 33, Harris used his immense popularity to travel far and wide discussing the progress of St. Louis schools. In turn, educators from across the United States (and in some cases, Europe) came to St. Louis to view the strategies in action. Down to the proper angle of hanging blackboards, Harris oversaw every operating facet of the St. Louis public school system.

Along with his push for improving facilities and operations, Harris also sought an elite teaching force. His primary concern was a teacher who was overworked, and one of his first priorities upon arriving in St. Louis was the shortening of the school week to five days from the existing six, and the provision of a two or two-and-a-half month vacation for teachers. In addition, Harris was able to lure quality teachers from other places to St. Louis by offering better salaries than what the teachers were receiving elsewhere – in some cases, as much as 120% (Leidecker, 1946). Although Cubberly (1912) cited this as the very reason that rural schools were not able to keep quality teachers for themselves, it nonetheless stocked the St. Louis schools with a veritable "Dream Team" of teachers near the turn of the century.

It interesting to note that Harris had little, if any, formal training in pedagogy. This was not unusual for school leaders in the late 1800s, however. Many superintendents, even in large districts (like Harris in St. Louis) had made their names in other fields. For Harris, his niche was carved out in the field of speculative philosophy. He was a devout pupil of the German philosopher Hegel, and was widely known as the leading Hegelian in the United States. As founder of the St. Louis Philosophical Society, he promoted Hegelian theory and the idea of the "will" in education. The will was the inner driving force that propelled one to become educated, and this occurred through an intensive study of the heritage of civilization. In the Hegelian definition of education, this heritage was comprised of "institutions" – school, church, family, etc. – which man used to further his knowledge of himself and his culture. Harris (along with colleague Henry Brockmeyer, who would later become the Lieutenant Governor of Missouri) was able to communicate the Hegelian creed to a wider audience through the gradual growth of the St. Louis Philosophical Society, an organization which Harris founded. In addition, Harris assumed the editor's role of the *Journal of Speculative Philosophy*, which he founded in 1867 and became arguably the first true philosophical journal in the United States.

As for the St. Louis curriculum, the teachers and students under Harris's scrutiny became immersed in what he sacredly referred to as the five "Windows to the Soul" – Grammar, Art and Literature, Geography, History, and Mathematics. "These are five substantial provinces of human learning which should be represented in the course of study at every stage of progress," he directed, "from the primary school up through the college" (1880, p. 171). Only through the concentrated study of these subjects could the inner-self be released, Harris believed. "To the school belongs in part this revealing of man to himself," he continued. "He may be educated and nourished by the spiritual food which is found only in this great revelation of man and realized in institutions and in the history of civilization" (ibid., p. 170). As part of this heritage to be studied, Harris commanded the retention of Latin and Greek in the core curriculum of the high school – Latin and Greek texts in their untranslated form, that is, as Harris believed that meaning from the great authors in those languages was lost in translations. He stated in no uncertain terms his feelings against student-centered curricula. "Rousseau's doctrine of a return to nature," he said, "must... seem to me the greatest heresy in educational doctrine" (1898, p. 37).

Innovations continued to flow during Harris's tenure in St. Louis, including the first public kindergarten in the United States under the direction of fellow Hegel follower Susan Blow. Nonetheless, some were beginning to consider his idealism a tough match in the fast-paced, quickly-changing world in the late nineteenth century. Many groups – now starting to call themselves "progressives" – began to challenge the ideas of strict traditional learning and curriculum. Harris retreated only slightly, however, and attempted to mesh the confusing new society with the time-honored subject matter that promoted his idea of "mental disciplinarianism." He would leave St. Louis in 1880 and later become the U.S. Commissioner of Education in 1889, a post he would hold until 1906.

The Committee of Ten

With this perceived rapid growth and change occurring in society, those involved in educational discussions on the national level feared a coming "fragmentation" of American schools. Despite the efforts of Mann, Barnard, and other crusaders for the common school movement, "formal schooling" was still a term that was loosely defined in the early 1890s. The slow movement of educational reform never seemed to reach some places, as familial instruction continued to dominate. Particularly in the rural South, the concept of using public money to support a local school system still met with resistance. What would help push reforms forward, it was imagined, was a comprehensive, "national" curriculum for schools to follow. It was believed that a universal curriculum would tidy up school systems already in place, as well as serve as an organizing principle in areas that were truly launching public schools for the first time. To produce such an important document, ten of the finest thinkers to be found were brought together for the decisions on what should be taught. The National Education Association initially called this group together in 1892. The primary functions of the "Committee of Ten," however, turned out to be the identification of some commonality in regard to college admission requirements, and decide to which degree high school students should be educated in each of the major subject areas – regardless of whether or not a student would pursue a college education.

Placed at the head of this group was Harris's ally Charles Eliot, who was serving as president of Harvard University. Despite his belief in the traditional curriculum, he was becoming known as a staunch supporter of a broadened course of studies at the collegiate level, particularly in the area of student electives. So, although inclined to support the maintenance of traditional subject matter, he was willing to embrace a certain degree of change for future curricular choices by students. According to Kliebard (1995a), "Eliot differed from most mental disciplinarians in that he thought that any subject, so long as it were capable of being studied over a long period, was potentially a disciplinary subject" (p. 10). Nonetheless he, like Harris, strongly endorsed the time-honored subjects as promoted by the Yale Faculty Report, and their camp became known as the *Humanists* (i.e., in belief of the "humanities" – not to be confused with the student-centered philosophies to become known as "Humanism" in the 1960s).

Being the prominent and highly-respected national figure in education that he was, Harris was an obvious choice for the committee as well. He was in the midst of his influential stretch as the U.S. Commissioner of Education, and it was wondered by some why he was not chosen to lead the committee instead of Eliot. In the end, it may be argued that Harris's dominance overpowered Eliot and the other committee members anyway. Kliebard (1995a) asserts that "Eliot, for example, had to settle for a choice of four different courses of study in the high school rather than the system of electives that he would have undoubtedly preferred" (ibid.). When asked about this topic, Harris made his position on student electives in the curriculum quite clear.

> The practice of offering to the pupil a choice between two or more courses of study – so-called "practical" and "classical" courses – is an occasion for the spread of error in regard to the functions of the branches of learning. It is not to be expected that the immature mind of youth can choose wisely in this most difficult of educational matters. (1880, pp. 174-175)

The other eight members of the committee included James Angell, President of the University of Michigan; John Tetlow, Headmaster of the Girls' High School and Latin Grammar School of Boston; James Taylor, President of Vassar College; Oscar Robinson, Principal of Albany (NY) High School; James Baker, President of the University of Colorado; Richard Jesse, President of the University of Missouri; James Mackenzie, Headmaster of the Lawrenceville (NJ) School; and Henry King, Professor of Education at Oberlin College. The group convened, along with a collection of advisors within each of the subject areas, at Columbia College in New York City November 9th through the 11th, 1892.

It was recommended by the committee that students choose one of four courses of study for graduation from high school, regardless of whether they were college-bound or not: the *Classical* course of study, which included three "foreign" languages (which may be characterized as "ancient" in contemporary terms), and one "modern" language (French, German, etc.); the *Latin-Scientific* course, which included two foreign languages and one modern; the *Modern* course, involving two modern languages; and the *English* course, involving one modern language. The committee also recommended the continuation of Latin and Greek as prominent parts of the curriculum, although the former was stressed more than the latter. Otherwise (and what became the report's greatest criticism), little else in the recommendations changed from the traditional curriculum as promoted by the Yale Faculty Report of 1828. Admittedly, the committee devoted most of its efforts to the construction of the Classical course, from which the other three courses were derived.

Although the four courses recommended by the Committee was designed to serve both college- and non-college bound students, many saw the plan as continuing to serve the needs of the college-bound only. Others discrepancies were also found, such as by Nicholas Murray Butler, at the time a young school administrator from New York. "Critical examination of the committee's programmes discloses grave defects in the most important of all, the Classical. It does not include continuous study in science, for that great department is not represented in the third year at all. History is similarly interfered with, and there would also be a break in the mathematical course if the option given in the fourth year were exercised in favor of history" (1894, p. 380).

The committee decided that unilateral direction on college admission requirements was not prudent; although it did "venture to suggest, in the interest of secondary schools, that uniform dates... be established for the admissions examinations of colleges and scientific schools throughout the United States" (NEA, 1893, p. 55). Here again, Butler (1894) felt that the committee was amiss by not making a recommendation on entrance standards. "The colleges have been injuring higher education in America by giving their own idiosyncrasies as to admission examinations free scope, instead of agreeing together upon a policy" (p. 382).

Approximately six months after the committee's report was made public, Eliot (1894) was asked what he thought was its most influential portion. "On the whole, the greatest promise of usefulness which I see in the Report of the Committee of Ten lies in its obvious tendency to promote cooperation among school and college teachers and all other persons intelligently interested in education" (p. 226). Ironically, the perceived perpetuation of the status quo – particularly in regard to the dominion of the college over other facets of American education – became the greatest detriment to the committee's work.

This feeling is sensed by Kliebard (1995a), who summarized the group's effort by noting that "as the twentieth century progressed, the Committee of Ten became a kind of symbol of the failure of the schools to react sufficiently to social change and the changing school population as well as to the crass domination exercised by the college over the high school" (p. 13).

Criticism also came from one of Harris's friends, W. H. Maxwell (1894), superintendent of the Brooklyn school system. "While admitting theoretically all that Dr. Harris claims for Greek and Latin," Maxwell chided, "I have yet to see that the high school does give this special power or training through the study of Greek... we can learn more of man as we found him in American life from our Teutonic forefathers than we can from Latin and Greek" (p. 153). Soon after, however, Harris humorously tortured his friend in a public debate on the issue. It was recorded as one of the great forensic moments in American education – in perhaps more ways than one. "When Dr. Harris was through, Mr. Marble [the moderator], in his inimitable manner, coolly moved that Mr. Maxwell be invited to ask Dr. Harris another question. But Mr. Maxwell was silent, impressively silent. Judge Draper, who sat behind him, nudged him repeatedly, and said so as to be heard far and near, 'Get up Maxwell, get up. Ask him another question.'

"To this, Mr. Maxwell replied, 'Get up yourself.'

"'Oh, I have a wife and children at home,' replied the Judge" (ibid.).

Harris indeed had become the undisputed champion of education and curriculum in the United States, and few dared to challenge his brilliance or reputation. Two years after the Committee of Ten report became public, the NEA asked him in 1895 to chair the Committee of Fifteen, a similar aggregation designed to re-evaluate the American elementary school curriculum. With Harris at the helm, what was produced was what was expected. It was recommended by the committee that the five prime subject areas – Harris' famous "Windows to the Soul" – continue to form the basis for elementary curriculum, albeit in scaled-down fashion. For example, in preparation for the advanced mathematics to be studied in high school, elementary students should have a thorough grounding in arithmetic (called "inorganic nature" by Harris); basic geography should precede geology and botany; basic history should precede "universal" history and civil government. In this way, the committee suggested, would there be a stronger link between the instruction in the lower and upper grade levels (Harris, 1895).

Herbartian Philosophy in American Curriculum

As the report of the Committee of Ten reached the channels of the American educational mainstream, it was clear that Harris and the other Humanists' desire to maintain the time-honored subjects in the curriculum was its most fervent message. Within the next couple of decades, they were confronted by a number of "movements" in the curriculum field. There were three most notable groups that positioned themselves to attempt to overtake the Humanists. To say that the three groups were "aligned" against the Humanists would be incorrect, for they also opposed one another in philosophy. However, they all had a common enemy in the old guard. One of the groups would directly challenge the Humanists immediately; the other two would make more of an impact in the 1920s and 1930s.

The most clear and present danger to the Humanists was a collection called the "Child-Study Developmentalists," who sought to harness the ever-growing body of knowledge on the natural development of the child, and use that information in the construction of a new curriculum for American schools. Another group, known as the "Social Efficiency" educators, wished to apply the new-found techniques of industry to the world of education, and in doing so eliminate the "waste" as was efficiently being done on the assembly lines of factories that were sprouting up across the land. This group saw its popularity rise in the first fifteen to twenty years of the new century. Finally, the "Social Meliorist" group was looking to denounce capitalism and rebuild society in the name of economic justice, with a curriculum and school system to match. This group would be bolstered by the hard times of the Great Depression in the 1930s, with their title and purpose evolving into the term "Reconstructionism," among other names.

In the background, but quietly influential, was yet another movement emerging on the American educational scene that sought to unseat the status quo. The theories of Johann Friedrich Herbart (1776-1841) had begun to take root with a number of educators in the United States, and were confronting the basic principles of *memoriter* learning. At the core of the Herbartian mode of learning was the process of moral development. This likened Herbart to fellow

European philosophers Herbert Spencer and Thomas Locke, who also viewed their contemporary educational systems as outdated and confining. In contrast to Locke and his *tabula rasa*, however, Herbart viewed the adolescent mind as active entity to shape itself, not a passive one to be filled with knowledge. As a result of moral education, Herbart concluded that children should develop strengths in five areas: inner freedom, perfection, benevolence, justice, and equity.

The focus on Herbart's philosophy of education also dealt with what was referred to as the "correlation of studies." A natural benefit was to be derived from an organized combination of subject matter. For centuries, the rote memorization of content had lent itself to the isolated examination of subjects; Herbart refuted this idea, and instead insisted that the correlation of studies would bring an "association of learning" to the knowledge presented. After his death, Herbart's ideas were forwarded by German educator Tuikson Ziller, who in 1856 founded the *Verein fur Wissenschaftliche Padagogik*, or later known as the Herbart Association. According to Charles DeGarmo (1896), it was Ziller who first advanced the prime Herbartian question for education, "How may instruction in the common school become an instrument for the development of moral character?" (p. 105).

Carrying the flag of the Herbartians in the United States was DeGarmo and brothers Charles and Frank McMurry, all of whom traveled to Germany in the last decade of the nineteenth century to study Herbart's philosophies firsthand. Excited to spread the word upon their return to the U.S., the trio founded The American Herbart Club in 1892, whose name later changed to the National Herbart Society and ultimately to the National Society for the Study of Education. The final generic term added to the organization's respectability and visibility on a national level, and Herbartian theory grew further.

The most important feature in the American translation of Herbartianism came in the idea of the "Correlation of Studies." The Herbartians, along with the other groups discussed, saw a continued stratification of high school subject areas after the Committee of Ten issued its report. For the traditional subject areas to have their full effect on students, the American Herbartians believed, a systematic, careful network of correlations needed to be devised within the curriculum. DeGarmo (1896) claimed that there were at least three prominent reasons – two psychological, and one ethical – that correlation was necessary. The psychological reasons acknowledged the egocentric tendencies of the student in relating subject matter to himself, and the application of subject matter by the student to his subsequent career(s). In an ethical sense, correlation would provide a greater moral foundation for students in their academic training, as had been traditionally believed in the German educational system. How, then, were American teachers supposed to pursue this? Charles McMurry (1901) offered some advice. "Cultivate in children all healthy appetites for knowledge, to set up interesting aims and desires at every step, to lead the approach to different fields of knowledge in the spirit of conquest…to implant vigorous aims and incentives in children is the great privilege of the teacher" (p. 67). As DeGarmo and the McMurry brothers involved themselves in the founding of normal schools across the Midwest in the late 1800s (such as those at present-day Northern Illinois University and Illinois State University), they were able to take their philosophies directly to those they were training for the teaching field.

John Dewey, Francis W. Parker, and Early Curriculum Studies
        As with a good number of other educators in the era, John Dewey was dissatisfied with the findings and recommendations of the Committee of Ten. Interestingly, however, much of Dewey's philosophical roots can be traced to Harris's with Hegelianism and the inner spirit of the individual. Like Harris, Dewey was a philosopher by training – not an educator. As he became noted in his writings on educational philosophy (and basically being credited with starting the Pragmatist movement), he was wooed by the various theoretical camps in curriculum to join their causes. Dewey did not feel, however, that any of the four major competing groups at the turn of the century (the Humanists, Child-Study Developmentalists, Social Efficiency Educators, or Social Meliorists) truly fit into what he believed should be a model for curriculum. Dewey did, however, subscribe to one unwavering stance – that a classroom is not a place that *trains students to live in a democracy*, but rather *is* a working, living democracy within itself, where different voices need to have equal power. Furthermore, he felt that the curriculum was not a fixed, static, concentrated body of knowledge, as the Humanists did; rather, it was a body that was constantly changing, being added to and taken from with the experiences that children brought to the arena of

learning. "Life outside the school," as Tyler (1949) lists as one critical source in the selection of objectives for the curriculum, was of the utmost importance for consideration, according to Dewey. It was upon this premise that he was brought to the University of Chicago in 1894 by university president William Rainey Harper to begin his lab school, one that would attempt to transform not only what people thought about curriculum, but also their conception of the entire teaching-and-learning process. Dewey would remain at Chicago for ten years, when a dispute in 1904 with Harper over university policies moved him to resign. The impact that was made, however, did cause a reconceptualization of what schooling could be.

On another front, more changes were taking place in the normal schools across the country – changes that would impact rural schools in particular. Cubberly (1912) noticed that "for the training of new teachers for the rural schools a number of normal schools have, within the past decade, organized rural teachers' training classes, provided a rural observation and practice school, and have offered special courses preparing directly for teaching in the rural schools" (p. 3). In the first decade of the 1900s, improvements were seen in all aspects of normal schools – not only in training for rural work. In 1900, only a fourth of the operating normal schools in the United States required a high school diploma for admission; within ten years, however, that percentage had climbed slowly to nearly a third. In 1908, the National Education Association passed a resolution in support of having *all* normal schools require a diploma for admission, something to which all institutions were complying by the early 1930s. The normal school concept, however, would soon be discarded in favor of a more comprehensive four-year college program of study. In 1920, there were 137 state normal schools and 46 teachers colleges in the United States. By 1933, the number of normal schools had decreased to 30, and the number of teachers' colleges had increased to 146 (Spring, 1986).

One educator at the turn of the century, in particular, sought an even greater progressive advance in teacher education. From the time that he entered his first classroom, Francis Wayland Parker was a rogue among academicians. The mental disciplinarian theories of Harris and the other Humanists did not sit well with Parker, and he sought to forge a new direction for the education of nation's teaching force. Parker himself was involved with the inquiries of the Committee of Ten, being part of the committee's Geography

Conference. With the debate about the American curriculum wide open in the early 1900s, Parker attempted to circulate new teacher-training strategies never conceptualized to the day.

A product of the New England countryside, Parker was born in New Hampshire in 1837 – two years after Harris, who was born in neighboring Connecticut. At the age of twenty-one, he moved to the Midwest and became headmaster of the school in Carrollton, Illinois. He called the experience "probably the roughest school in which I ever taught" (Rippa, 1992) and was rescued from the ordeal by the outbreak of the American Civil War, in which he served to the duration and achieved the rank of colonel – a title which he proudly kept throughout his academic life as well.

Rote memorization and content-driven teaching methods – at the very soul of the traditional school and curriculum advocated by Harris – was viewed as nearly useless by Parker. In contrast to his contemporaries, he abandoned the application of corporal punishment and felt that only poor teachers used such techniques (Parker, 1899). It was while teaching in Dayton, Ohio that he began to study pedagogy, and thus began his pursuits of finding better ways to teach and motivate young people. Like Dewey, Parker pushed for the idea that the child and the curriculum are inseparable; that the two entities should not mutually exclude each other simply because they were "opposing, unnatural" furies. He especially believed in utilizing the natural curiosity that was within each young student. "Perhaps the most marked mental action of the little child," he once noted, "is the fanciful creation of new ideas and images" (1894, p. 4).

Parker used the financial opportunity of an inheritance to travel and study in Europe. While abroad, he became fascinated with the teachings of Herbart and Pestalozzi. Increasingly convinced that education should drift away from subject-matter specifics and towards the child himself, Parker returned to the United States in 1875 with a new outlook on the teaching-and-learning process. Long an admirer of Horace Mann, Parker assumed a principal's position in Quincy, Massachusetts, in the backyard of Mann's roots. It was Parker's self-admitted "opportunity of a lifetime"; he dismantled the Quincy curriculum and installed a child-centered program, one in which the teachers abandoned traditional texts and encouraged the students to bring in more reading material from home. The Quincy school discovered a new excitement for learning, for both faculty and students; suddenly, the learning that was going on appeared to be more relevant to the students' lives. The concept of "Object Teaching," made famous from the theories of Pestalozzi, began to take hold as well. All in all, the new situation in the school became known as the "Quincy Plan" for teaching, and soon was famous throughout the Northeast and beyond.

In a curricular sense, Parker stressed a broad range of subjects for study. In addressing the natural curiosity that lay within each child, it was then up to the teacher to provide a stimulus – however remote it may originally appear to be – that would stoke academic fervor in his studies. In the typical litmus test, the students of Quincy were ultimately sent up against their inevitable challenge – their performance on the state exams of Massachusetts with their peers from other schools. Not surprising to Parker, his students met or exceeded the performance of other students around the state. "If you asked me to name the best of all results, I should say," Parker noted, "the more humane treatment of little folks... the rod was well-nigh banished. The doctrine of total depravity will have much to answer for on the day of judgement." (Parker, 1902) He believed fully in the simple grace and natural purity of the child, and that proper nurturing would unleash the power within.

Parker arrived in Chicago in 1883 after a three-year stint as superintendent of the Boston schools. He envisioned the job as an opportunity to do, on a broader scale, the work he had done in Quincy. Unexpectedly (to him), he had met political turbulence in Boston, and thus never was able to attain complete control of his school. He found that his ideas, so workable in the smaller city of Quincy, faced problems in the larger metropolitan area. His relatively brief stint in Quincy (five years), however, had left a lasting impression in New England, and he sought new ground to conquer. He took his love for children to the Midwest, and in the process set up a new outlet for his ideas at the Cook County Normal School in Chicago. Like Dewey, Parker believed that the school was not a *training ground* for a democracy; rather, that a full-fledged democracy existed within the classroom itself. One of his more famous phrases to his pre-service teachers, in fact, was that "a school should be a model home, a complete community and embryonic democracy." Students brought in ideas, problems, observations, hypotheses, etc., that not only contributed to the classroom environment but also built the curriculum. Like Mann, Parker believed that the foundation of American democracy was a common education system for the nation's citizens. Mann called the idea of common schools "the balance wheel of the social machinery"; Parker called it "the cohesive element in a free society."

While in the midst of building the Cook County Normal School for training teachers, Parker developed a strong friendship with Dewey upon the latter's arrival at the University of Chicago in 1894. A large piece of freedom also arrived for Parker when, just before the turn of the century, control of the normal school was relinquished by the Cook County Board and given to the University of Chicago. This provided much relief, as he was beginning to envision a similar political battle for autonomy that he had waged in Boston. When this break with county board occurred, Parker was able to work directly with Dewey and his lab school. The two complemented one another incredibly well, and Dewey used Parker's school as a combined experiment with his own. Parker set up a "practice school" that was attached to his normal school, and the children of the neighborhood in which the normal school was located began attending it. In addition, Dewey had many of his students simultaneously enroll in the practice school as well as his lab school.

Parker was, in essence, the first American educator on the national scene to promote rural areas as a genuine source of curricular material. Parker envisioned the traditional American farm – the very essence of rural life – as the perfect basis for the rural school curriculum. Speaking about his visits with a boy in an agrarian section of New Hampshire, Parker (NEA, 1901) noted how the needs for every subject were met within the setting of the family property – and that ultimately, the boy would wait too long in life to make use of the things he had learned.

> At eight years of age, he began to study – study in the best sense of that much-abused word. He began the study of geography... he studied botany... he studied zoology... he had a practical knowledge of meteorology... in fact, every subject now known in the curriculum of the university this boy studied in an elementary way. He lived to become a school-teacher, and taught school earnestly and bunglingly for twenty years before he had even a suspicion of the value of his farm life and farm work. (p. 528)

Furthermore, Parker breaks down each component of the "farm curriculum" into individual elements. The boy's geography lessons included investigations of hills, valleys, springs, and swamps; within the study of botany, the nature of different grasses, herbs, weeds and grains served as the matter of inquiry. In his examination of meteorological tendencies, the boy developed knowledge in patterns of atmospheric conditions that "could foretell storms with nearly as much wisdom as is exercised by the Weather Bureau" (p. 529). While cautioning the reader that such a curriculum requires much fine-tuning, Parker nonetheless asserts that this plan "can form the substantial basis for all study" in rural schools nationwide (ibid.) The subject upon which Parker laid the most criticism of traditional practitioners was geography. He found it imperative that children take trips into the "field," run mud models through their hands, and draw their own impressions of landscapes in order to fully understand the nature of the environment (Pinar, et al., 1995). Nachtigal (1992) strikes a similar note with Parker in contemporary times, as he believes that "rural schools have ready access to a living laboratory for science right outside the school door" (p. 86). And Cubberly (1912) asserted that it was due time for the American school curriculum to be adjusted "more fully to the needs of country life" (p. 4).

Upon Parker's death in 1902, his normal school and Dewey's lab school consolidated and formed what became known as the School of Education at the University of Chicago. The undergraduate training was carried out by the Education school, while graduate work in education fell under the auspices of the Department of Philosophy. Dewey took command of both areas, and his surge in power ultimately led to the conflict with President Harper, and Dewey resigned in 1904.

Summary

Remaining neither approached or reconsidered for over fifty years, the traditional curriculum found its pinnacle of influence in American schools in the 1800s. It had been validated by the works of two major influential groups – the Yale Faculty Report of 1828 and the Committee of Ten on Secondary Education in 1893 (coinciding with the Committee of Fifteen on Elementary Education in 1895). With rapid changes in society occurring as the 1900s approached, however, educational reformers viewed the actions of the latter group to insufficiently meet the diverse needs of students in the new century. A number of opposing philosophies began to emerge, as some educators sought to "free" the student from the perceived constraints of the time-honored subject matter. Being so firmly entrenched, however, the traditional group – known as the "Humanists" for their staunch support of the humanities – withstood the attacks, led by the indomitable William Torrey Harris.

As Kliebard (1995a) frankly noted, "The preeminent figure in the world of education during the last quarter of the nineteenth century was undoubtedly Harris... Harris's basic position in curriculum matters continued to hold sway with the majority of teachers and administrators across the country for years to come" (pp. 30-31).

If nothing else, the reformers did awaken the academe to the need for flexibility in the changing times. An epic example of this societal change was seen in mass exodus of rural residents to the job-rich cities at the turn of the century. This population shift propelled the assembly of yet another national committee on curriculum as the 1900s came to a close. This group, as a cousin of its predecessors, would come to be known as the "Committee of Twelve on the Rural School Problem," and would attempt to address inconsistencies that were apparent in rural school instruction nationwide.

3. A National Imposition on Rural Curriculum: The Committee of Twelve, 1897

In the love of home, the love of country has its rise.

– Charles Dickens

As in modern times, certain similar demographics were present in many American rural communities in the 1890s. These areas often possessed common qualities such as a homogeneous religious or racial composition, intimate knowledge of local news and events, or perhaps a singular source of employment for the local workforce, such as milling, mining, agriculture, etc. However, due to this similarity, the mistaken assumption was made by "mainstream" America that her rural areas maintained similar *moral* structures. Like today, differences in the moral cultures of American small towns in the 1890s created distinctions of educational policy and curricular philosophy for their schools. Nonetheless, prominent educators over history have often attempted – either subtly or overtly – to implement a national curriculum for rural schools in the United States, envisioning a consistent "product" emerging when graduates leave *any* small-town school system. The most notable and formative of these efforts occurred between the years 1897 and 1918, as the entire nation grappled with a swiftly changing social and economic base. This era preceded the more systemic, national reforms in curriculum later in the twentieth century, in which rural schools played an active role in their formation and delivery.

Not long after the dust had settled from the Committee of Ten, another collection of scholars – twelve, this time – was appointed in July 1895 by the National Council of Education to investigate the state of rural schools in the United States. This committee, which included the influential input of Harris, produced reports that were presented at the 1897 meeting of the National Education Association. In the midst of a society that was experiencing widespread industrialization, the "Committee of Twelve on the Rural School Problem" recommended measures that would attempt to standardize the efforts of schools in the agrarian sector. Each of the measures – such as consolidation, the re-training of teachers for the unique circumstances of rural education, and the procurement of common libraries, among others – impacted the course that the local curriculum would take in each rural school system. The resulting documents were designed to provide approximate templates for districts to follow. It was envisioned that a standardized rural school system in the United States would serve as an efficient complement to an expanding urban population.

The rural school situation was indeed seen as a "problem" by most urban educators and, according to Nachtigal (1982), the remedies that the committee prescribed included "consolidation of schools and transportation of pupils, expert supervision by county superintendents, taking the schools out of politics, and professionally trained teachers" (p. 16). Furthermore, Theobald (1995) asserts that "the committee pushed the Herbartian notion that education ought to be driven by the child's interests and that in so doing the unstable American society of the 1890s might benefit" (p. 162). Others saw the "problem" as something greater in scope, as stated by Cubberly (1912). "One mistake that has been made in dealing with the rural school problem is the assumption that it is a problem by itself, instead of being but a part of a much larger problem affecting the conditions of rural and village life" (p. 10). The Committee of Twelve sought to alleviate difficulties that affected both rural schools and rural life in general. Or as Schubert (1980) described the scene, "The new emphasis on curriculum was developed and implemented in each of the thousands of little red schoolhouses that dotted the American countryside" (p. 46).

However, when many of the committee's recommendations reached the local level, the interpretations were significantly influenced by the local flavor of each rural community. Consequently, the transformed curriculum comprised less conformity to the national expectations and more of a reflection of the values and needs of the particular school system. It is interesting to note that presentations at subsequent NEA meetings most prominently displayed this localism; throughout the meetings of the early 1900s, rural principals and superintendents returned to discuss how the policies affected their individual curricula and the resulting convergence of the Committee of Twelve's recommendations and their communities' own value structures. Thus, the question may be asked: to what extent, and to what degrees, did national rural school policy get transformed into local curriculum during this period?

The Committee of Twelve divided itself into four sub-committees of three members apiece, each of which investigated a specific concern for the future of the rural school curriculum. These categories included School Maintenance, Supervision, The Supply of Teachers, and Instruction and Discipline (National Education Association, 1897). Henry Sabin, Superintendent of the Des Moines, Iowa public schools, served as chairman. Sabin and his colleagues summarized the reports of the four sub-committees by producing seven general recommendations for all rural schools:

1. The county or township is the most desirable size of school governance.

2. Local financial support of schools should continue, supplemented by the state.

3. Widespread consolidation of smaller rural schools should occur.

4. Normal school training should focus on issues of rural school settings.

5. Adequate libraries for rural areas should be constructed.

6.   Rural schools require the presence of qualified supervision and administration.

7. The rural school should remain a place of learning moral and patriotic values (NEA, 1897).

In addition to the committee's summary, however, other nationally-known educators were furnishing their own recommendations for the re-structuring of the rural school curriculum.   Emerson White, in his report entitled "The Country School Problem," also suggested that the standardization of the rural school across the United States would lead to a desirable, standardized rural school curriculum.   To form the basis for this curriculum, White recommended the following   reforms for the operations of all rural schools: 1)   An emphasis on *sequence* (as opposed to scope) within the curriculum, as most rural schools are likely to enroll students with diverse ages and ability ranges and 2) the limitation of the rural school day to six hours of total instruction time, as work responsibilities for both teachers and students outside of school are often exhaustive in agrarian settings (NEA, 1897).

To achieve these goals, White proposed the implementation of the "Three-Grade Programme," in which the "A-Grade" pupils would complete eight exercises each day, the "B-Grade" pupils six exercises, and the "C-Grade" pupils five.   These grades would be further subdivided into smaller classifications.   Rather than conceptualizing the three "grades" in the traditional sense, White suggested that these are the three *stages* that a student passes through from early instruction through secondary school.   In fact, he recommends that the terms "groups" or "sections" be used instead. The reasons for dividing the pupils into three sections, White contended, were threefold: the necessary freedom of classification and instruction in each section, a standard of evidence for progress, and a needed reduction of class exercise*s* in writing, drawing, language, and other school arts in which *skill* is the chief end (p. 542).

Lawton Evans, Superintendent of the Richmond County (GA) schools, also issued recommendations for standardizing rural school policy across the nation (NEA, 1897).   In echoing the edict set forth by the Committee of Twelve, Evans suggested that the county system of organization was the most efficient and would produce a curriculum that best suited the needs of all residents in a given area.

He advocated continuing the nine-month calendar, to be adjusted to the harvest-time needs of particular areas. In addition, he advised that all schoolhouses be situated no more than an average of four miles apart, so as to allow all children to be within walking distance of their schools. Furthermore, he recommended that each schoolhouse be owned by the county board of education, to cost within the range of $300-$2,500 (depending on size and materials needed), and that one superintendent should have charge over all of the schools in the county. Evans' suggestions prompted a curriculum for the Richmond County schools that sought to unite all of the students in the county under a single system of learning, thus abandoning the individual curricula of local towns that had flourished beforehand. The premise that Evans was trying to forward had support from other educators, however, such as Cubberly (1912). "It is only by a state and county-wide pooling of effort, to maintain what is for the common good of all, that good schools can be maintained throughout a state" (p. 22). Cubberly claimed that lessons learned from county organization in other facets of government should be incorporated in the rural school system. "In most other public functions – assessment and taxation, poor-relief, roads and bridges, sanitation, control of the liquor traffic, the administration of justice, and in some matters, for schools also, the county is the prevailing unit, and to add the schools to the list would be a good addition" (pp. 41-42).

Prescriptions for rural school curriculum, therefore, also came from urban educators, whose interests and experiences were often quite removed from rural areas. As another example, Fannie Dunn, professor at the City Teachers College of New York, saw the rural elementary curriculum as requiring four crucial components: the promotion of individual and community health, the study of selecting and consuming social products, the study of civic and social duties, and the study of various forms of recreation (NEA, 1921). The conception of the rural school situation as being *problematic* (seen again, as stated in the very title of the "Committee of Twelve on the Rural School *Problem*") appeared to give urban educators the license to offer suggestions as to its improvement. Solutions to the "problems" were being enlisted from all available sources, including experts in education who were outside of rural areas. A prejudice, in fact, had become the predominant view: that educated people in rural areas were actually uneducated, and needed the assistance of urban educators in the organization of their school systems.

In this vein, particular textbooks that were deemed appropriate for use in rural schools were being widely distributed into the 1900s. The curriculum that formed around these textbooks often served to reinforce the impoverished, backwards stereotype of the agrarian student, in comparison with his or her presumably more affluent, cultured urban counterpart. For example, Theobald (1993) cites a *McGuffey Reader* from the period that was specifically designed for rural boys. "When he sees little boys or girls riding on pretty horses, or walking with ladies and gentlemen, and having on very fine clothes, he does not envy them or wish to be like them" (p. 121). Such passages not only submerged the rural student in a self-image of poverty but also infused the same bias in the thoughts of mainstream America as well.

The problem, however, was not limited to the actual curriculum and instruction being utilized in the rural schoolhouses. The Committee of Twelve also viewed the adjustment of the normal school curriculum to be critical to the understanding and execution of the rural school curriculum by prospective teachers. In addition to an improved teaching corps, the need for better supervision and administration in rural schools was also made a priority, as was noted in studies that followed in subsequent decades (see Holloway, 1928; Burton and Barnes, 1929). The Supply of Teachers subcommittee produced a guide for the training of teachers for positions in rural areas. Subjects to be studied in the normal school included school economy, school psychology, literature, mathematics, history, science, and several others. At first glance, such a curriculum may appear to be basic to any normal school setting; however, the committee recommended that these courses be taught to pre-service teachers in a mode that would correspond to the typical needs of rural settings. For example, the study of botany would include the elements of agriculture, cash crops, and other concepts associated with farming; the examination of school economy would focus on the specific monetary concerns of small schools; the study of literature would highlight the contributions of rural writers to the field (NEA, 1897).

The Committee of Twelve noted that teachers in rural areas were often poorly-trained, unprofessional, and in some cases, even partially or fully illiterate. Despite the committee calling for sweeping national changes in normal school training to alleviate this problem, the matter of providing qualified teachers for understanding and transmitting the unique rural curriculum often fell to the individual states. It was decided that the states had to form their own plans to meet their particular needs in this regard. This was exemplified by "The State of Maine Plan," as presented by Augustus Thomas, State Superintendent of Public Instruction in Augusta, Maine. Seeking individuals who would improve and promote the local curriculum in rural areas, the 1919 Maine legislature provided funds for the selection of 100 graduates of normal schools for six weeks of training in problems common to rural curriculum and instruction. At the end of their first year of teaching, graduates of the program received a bonus of one-fourth their base salary. Upon completing the program, the state dispersed the 100 teachers equally throughout the state, and directed them to pursue improvement of the local curriculum in their areas (NEA, 1920).

The Advent of Consolidation

The most sweeping reform advocated by the Committee of Twelve, and the one which consequently took on the most diverse local flavor, was school consolidation – the incorporation of smaller township schools into larger ones. Upon its recommendation, the policy almost unilaterally altered each rural school system across the country. If a school was too small, it was closed and its students sent to a larger, neighboring community; if a school was larger than the average, it was seen as having the accommodations to take in students from the smaller areas – notwithstanding the physical capacity of its schoolhouse. Naturally, this policy encountered local problems that were unique to the various settings. In his report to the NEA in 1903 (six years after the Committee of Twelve recommendations), John Prince of the Massachusetts State Board of Education became the first to publicly acknowledge the various dilemmas associated with the consolidation template. He suggested that the idea of wholesale consolidation for rural schools might not be the most appropriate for all areas of the nation.

> While it must be admitted that great good has been accomplished in the past by the closing of small schools and the transportation of the pupils to other schools, and while the testimony seems to favor an extension of such a plan, it may well be questioned whether it is desirable for

all the rural schools, even for all the small rural schools, to be consolidated. (p. 933)

Prince warned against the local difficulties that may occur due to the removal of local school control – difficulties that would differ in severity with respect to the nature of the area and the stake that the residents held in their schools. Citing the most basic of examples, Prince discussed the increased distance of traveling to school for the student enrolled in the consolidated school. Laws in Ohio and Pennsylvania required free transportation to any consolidated student living over three-fourths of a mile away, whereas in Kansas, the minimum distance for a free ride to school was two miles. Prince continued by pointing out that no individual system of consolidation within a given state could be viewed as a model for others to follow.

> Being assured of the possibilities for good in the consolidation of rural schools, we next have to inquire how best it may be accomplished. Shall the local school board, as in Massachusetts, Ohio, and New Jersey, be given full authority to consolidate the schools and to transport the pupils; or shall it be subject to certain legal restrictions, such, for example, as exist in Indiana, where the trustees of a school district may act only upon petition of a majority of the voters; or as in New Hampshire, where only a certain percentage of the school money may be expended for the conveyance of pupils; or as in Rhode Island, where schools only may be closed that have an average membership of less than twelve; or as in Iowa, where the boards are limited in their appropriation for transportation to five dollars for each person of school age? (p. 931)

Even looking solely at Prince's examples, it is evident that the impact of consolidation brought individual and unique problems to different areas of the country. Within the basic framework of the consolidation plan, the students of rural America were being asked to play the same game by different rules; the lack of congruence among national policy, state law, and local need became an inherent predicament. Naturally, transportation of students arose as a large issue as well, the disparity of which was later brought to the fore by the writings of Butterworth and Dawson (1952). "Approximately half the states specify the distance from school that makes the provision of transportation service by the district desirable or necessary. This distance varies from one mile in Louisiana to four miles in South Dakota" (p. 390). Thus, in terms of seeking a universal policy on consolidation, the states were not even in agreement on how far a student should be traveling to school.

The storm of consolidation that rode over the Midwest in the early 1900s was perhaps most clearly visible in the state of Ohio. E. A. Jones, the State Commissioner of Common Schools in Ohio, noted the dramatic increase of consolidated townships, beginning with Kingsville in 1892. In 1898, Ohio school boards were given the power to reduce the number of operating school buildings under their jurisdictions. By 1900, 17 more townships had joined Kingsville as consolidated districts; in 1901, the total number rose to 46; in 1902, 70; and by 1907, the number had increased to 157 total townships consolidated (NEA, 1908). Students began traveling to larger, neighboring communities for their schooling, and in most cases they encountered a more broad-based curriculum in place, with courses (particularly in the languages and sciences) that were previously unavailable to them. However, as illustrated by Fleming (1995), the consolidated curriculum was not well-received by parents in the annexed communities in Ohio; a feeling of compromise pervaded many, as the new, strange, and enlarged curriculum that their children were now undertaking was a venture outside of their known local structure.

As this attempted standardization of rural school policy continued to settle on individual districts across the country, the recommendations were met with suspicion. Townspeople were generally unwilling to relinquish their voices in curriculum matters, as a mistrust grew of "outsiders" who, local residents believed, sought to bring a replicated, manufactured school product to every rural community. This defensiveness was displayed in one place by W.H. Campbell, Chairman of the Committee on Education of the Farmers' Educational and Cooperative Union of Central City, Nebraska (NEA, 1917). Campbell stressed the need to maintain local power in rural curriculum formation and called on the people in such places to take action. "If this is truly a government by the people," he noted, "they must be alive and shape their own school system to meet their individual and their community needs... a ready-made plan [for all rural schools] has never worked and never will work" (p. 600). Campbell also pointed out that the needs of rural schools must be acknowledged within all local regions of the United States. That perspective rebuffed the suggestion of the "county system" of school organization seen earlier (presented by Lawton Evans of Georgia) as Campbell continued:

> There is the plan called the "county unit" of administration, which has been legislated upon in some states and rejected by others. In some states where people never took the initiative in government or had no desire to do so, this plan may work; but out in the great Middle West, it has been rejected as autocratic, centralizing too much power in the hands of a few and weakening the initiative and the spirit of the people. (p. 601)

It is interesting here to note the "sectionalism" of rural school interests in the United States at this point in history. The county plan, as suggested by Evans, was perhaps constructed to serve the more densely-populated states of the eastern part of the country. However, as in the case with Campbell and his home territory of Nebraska, it was feared that school systems in states on the frontier with more isolated towns would fall victim to a "dictatorial" system of organization in which those without political leverage in sparsely-populated areas succumb more easily to the decisions made at the county level.

Florence Hale, State Agent for Rural Education (and assistant to Thomas) in Augusta, Maine, also noted the need for local control in spite of national policy (NEA, 1915). "To make standardization of rural schools possible, the standard rating sheet and the whole plan must be simply and clearly put up to the people of the community" (p. 287). With many of their fellow farmers, mill workers, and coal miners leaving the area to take more lucrative jobs in the cities, many rural residents saw the educational reforms proposed by national figures as the beginning of the end – the ultimate, inevitable encroachment of the city population (and way of life) on the countryside.

Despite the call by the Committee of Twelve to expand school libraries and other public reading resources for children, the amount of reading that took place in most rural schools actually remained in accordance with the amount of reading material available to the student in his or her home. Charles Holley, in his report "The Relationship between Persistence in School and Home Conditions," examined the reading practices of children in rural areas of central Illinois. His study revealed that students in this region remained in school longer, their stay was more successful, and they were able to more willfully embrace the school curriculum when coming from homes where more books were present (NSSE, 1914). In many rural homes, only wealthy families were privileged to maintain large private libraries. This discrepancy also helped shape the rural school curriculum, as schools without funds for textbooks would request that students bring whatever reading material they could from home.

The report of the Committee on Relations of Public Libraries to Public Schools, authored by Charles McMurry, Frank Hutchins, and others, also noted the inequity that existed in the number of volumes available to rural schools nationwide (NEA, 1899). The committee sent out questionnaires to the supervisors of libraries in communities of 2,500 or less, asking for the amount and quality of available resources in their particular townships. The replies received by the committee led them to believe that "the pupils in only a very few states have respectable library facilities, and that a great population have none" (p. 507). The Committee of Twelve had called for the improvement of township and school libraries in all rural sectors, but a large disparity appeared to remain. McMurry's committee (NEA, 1899) went on to note:

> Nearly all of the villages in New England and New York have free public libraries, and, although many of them are poorly managed, the library associations and library commissions in those states are rapidly improving them. In the states mentioned and in Michigan, Wisconsin, Minnesota, New Jersey, Montana, and California, where the states aid rural-school libraries, nearly every school has a library, and these libraries are growing in size and improving in quality. In a few other northern states quite a proportion of the schools have fair libraries, and, occasionally, there are some notable school libraries.

> It may be fairly said that in no state in the Union have all, or nearly all, the children in rural communities adequate

school- and public-library facilities, and that in fully half of the states pupils do not have free access to suitable collections of books. (p. 507)

Although not listed as one of the seven specific recommendations by the Committee of Twelve, the suggestion for widespread maintenance of agricultural education also resounded throughout the report. Ironically, it is within this area of study that the rural curriculum undertook its *most* localized form, as varying conditions (both environmental and educational) in different areas served to alter the form that agricultural instruction assumed in a given community. Josiah Main, professor at the Oklahoma Agricultural and Mechanical College in Stillwater, noted (NEA, 1914) that "every school has done what was right in its own eyes at the expense of the disciplinary and preparatory values of the subject" (p. 809). He suggested that no two of the fifty best agricultural education programs in the state of Oklahoma were alike, and thus no overriding policy at the national level (let alone the state level) should be imposed on its use. Even the year-to-year differences within the *same community* are not discernible in agricultural education, as "there is no unifying principle by the application of which the school man can determine in what year and in what order of sequence animal husbandry, or soils, or field crops, or a half-dozen others are best given" (p. 808).

To further understand the localized nature of agricultural education during the period, one may examine the "Junior Club" programs being instituted a thousand miles away from Oklahoma in the rural school systems of Maryland. The concept of the Junior Club, an organization designed to connect the classroom experiences of the agrarian child to the physical world, was considered a prelude to the modern-day 4-H clubs across the United States. According to Frances Clark (NEA, 1921), an educator in the Easton, Maryland school system, agricultural projects carried out in the Junior Club had effectively served as the organizing principle for the curriculum of the Easton schools; projects that were developed through the natural outdoor activities of the students. "In order to stimulate the child's interest in Junior Club work as the teacher views the situation, motives which govern the choice of projects must be worked out by the child" (p. 564). Through use of the activities and projects developed in the Junior Club, rural schools in Maryland sought to correlate reading, writing, and arithmetic with agriculture and home economics; this correlation was seen to develop the most "interest and pleasure in school work as a whole" (p. 564). Not far away in Montgomery County, Maryland, County Superintendent Nat Brogden (NEA, 1915) noted that despite the recommendations given by the Committee of Twelve, two prime essentials remained critical to the curriculum of the schools in his jurisdiction: the development of projects that have their origins in the special experiences of Montgomery County and the local methods, knowledge, and life experiences that have been nurtured by the residents of the area, and in turn passed on to the contemporary students of the county.

The concept of industrial education was seen as another natural part of the rural school curriculum in all areas of the country. Industrial skills (often interchanged – perhaps mistakenly – with "vocational" skills) were assumed as going hand-in-hand with agricultural traits, as the economy of most rural communities centered around farming, milling, or mining work. Even as universal as this concept appeared to be throughout the land, however, the endorsement of a model program for use in the local schools, as with other items suggested by the Committee of Twelve, brought its own interpretation within different states and townships. In its 1907 report to the NEA, the National Council of Education noted the lack of a bona fide plan in many states for industrial education in their rural areas; and in states where such plans were present, the courses of study for rural students differed greatly. The state of Maine, for example, had no provision for training in industrial education within its normal schools; furthermore, the state superintendent held the power to implement any course of study in industrial training he saw fit. In New Hampshire, on the contrary, "The local school board is supreme in all matters relating to [industrial education] in the common schools, and the function of the state superintendent is, in the main, purely advisory" (p. 130). What each individual state and community considered as acceptable training in the industrial arts differed greatly, due in large part to whatever happened to be the dominant industry of the local area.

Yet another implicit recommendation within the document of the Committee of Twelve was the general improvement of health conditions in rural areas, and the provision for health instruction in the curriculum of all agrarian schools. As with the other recommendations made, however, the actual implementation of this policy only went as far as the resources and instructional tendencies of a given area would carry it – along with legislative influence at the state level. G.W. Ager, Superintendent of the Jackson County (OR) Schools, noted that improved health and health education became among the most prominent demands by people in the rural sections of Oregon (NEA, 1920), and the state legislature responded with a law that made "twenty minutes of physical instruction and drill compulsory in all public schools" (p. 273). However, the ability of local school systems to employ physical education instructors, nurses, and other critical personnel for student well-being differed in various places. Thus (as with many such situations today), the stipulations of legislation for schools were often met with difficulty in some far-reaching rural corners of certain states.

Perhaps the most positive aspect of the Committee of Twelve report was a heightened awareness of the need for wider offerings in the rural school curriculum. "Modern conditions require a broader and more thorough education than that demanded by former times," announced Betts (1913). "And far more than the typical district rural school affords. The old-time school offered only the "three R's," and this was thought sufficient for an education. But these times have passed" (pp. 57-58). Indeed, with the efforts of programs like the Junior Club in Maryland and other vocational projects, the rural curriculum had expanded. But there was more work to be done. "The curriculum offered is pitifully narrow even for an elementary school," Betts continued, "and very few high schools are supported by rural communities. In fact, a large proportion of our rural population are receiving an education but little in advance of that offered a hundred years ago in similar schools" (pp. 58-59).

Resulting in part from the minimal efficacy of the Committee of Twelve's recommendations, a new attempt at rural curriculum standardization commenced in 1920. The constitution and by-laws were drafted for the new "Department of Rural Education" within the NEA. The creation of this department was seen as a fresh beginning in the construction of rural school curriculum and policy. In concept, the DRE was a mild reformation of its predecessors, the Department of Agricultural Education (1907), the Department of Rural and Industrial Education (1908), and the Department of Rural and Agricultural Education (1909-1919). The DRE published its mission statement in 1921, including the future vision for rural schools "that curricula be developed offering vocational courses in home-training for girls and in agriculture for boys with a broad general high-school course" (p. 527).

Certain policy recommendations that affected rural curriculum carried over from the Committee of Twelve to the DRE objectives, the most notable of which continued to be widespread consolidation. As transportation to far-away schools was just as problematic for many in 1921 as it was in 1897, the DRE listed accessibility to consolidated locations as an urgent priority for isolated areas. "We advocate increased efforts toward consolidation as one of the most important means to adequate rural education and commend good-roads programs as essential to successful consolidation" (p. 527). The conglomerating urban sector of American society was still influencing the rural sector into the 1920s, as the industrial model of "mass production" leaked into the formation of school structure; the notion of "bigger being better" was well on its way towards overwhelming most societal institutions.

In a truly historic proposal for school policy, the DRE called for the qualified teacher to be at the center of curriculum planning for agrarian schools. "We stress the importance of a rural-school curriculum, broad in its social content, rich in its cultural resources, adapted to the life of the child, and developed by a teacher whose professional insight and skill shall be the first requisites in her preparation" (p. 526). It is reasonable to extrapolate that "teacher" in the passage above refers not only to the actual classroom teacher, but a principal, superintendent, or other supervisory officials as well. Nonetheless, the recommendation marked an initial empowerment of the professional educator in the rural school curricular scene, a landscape once dominated exclusively by local wishes and values. The common school teacher, previously viewed as an uneducated pawn in the community, now commanded more power and respect than ever before.

Summary

The period between 1897 and 1921 was an era of great change in American society. The ascension of industry, immigration, and the economy in general permanently altered the paradigms of living in the United States, as the "factory model" of organization began to dominate not only the business sectors of the nation but educational spheres as well. Rural communities and rural schools were left in the wake of this rapid social change, as educators, politicians, and other community leaders were distraught with the task of managing the great numbers flocking to the employment-rich American cities. In what might even be viewed as an *afterthought* about the state of American rural education, the Committee of Twelve of 1897 provided a unilateral template for the restructuring of the rural school curriculum – a restructuring which, in formulating a common guide for all such schools to follow, would presumably provide the entire nation with a reliable social product (student) from rural education. In the construction of its recommendations, however, the suggestions offered by the committee did not take into account the local cultures of the various rural communities across the country – cultures nearly as numerous as the communities themselves. When implementing the recommendations by the Committee, rural school teachers and administrators often discovered an uneasy fit in their particular areas. The cultures of individual rural areas came to the fore in the subsequent reports to the NEA and consequently emitted a localized interpretation of what were intended to be universal curricular policies.

The recommendation of the Committee that carried the greatest impact was consolidation. This movement would be bolstered in the 1950s and '60s by the writings of James Conant, who viewed the curriculum of the small, unconsolidated rural school as inadequate for the needs of contemporary society. As transportation and communication technologies continued to improve throughout the century, further consolidation of rural schools appeared to many educators to be a reasonable route for curricular progress. However, shifts in the procedural focus of curriculum development continued throughout the century due to factors other than consolidation. Discrepancies over content and process – as well decision-making power in content and process – made curriculum development projects more complex than ever before. This complexity obscured, to a certain extent, the roles of teachers in these projects as the United States entered the 1920s. Teachers, school administrators, and the general public – from both urban and rural sectors alike – would now be vaulted into yet another era of curriculum reform, as more voices joined the debate on the appropriate subject matter for the schools.

4. Social-Efficiency Curriculum and the Changing Rural Landscape, 1918-1950

Hardly a competent workman can be found who does not devote a considerable amount of time to studying just how slowly he can work.

— Frederick Taylor

Some viewed the efforts of the Committee of Twelve as having very little effect on the status of rural schools. "The result is that, after almost two decades of agitation," Ellwood Cubberly noted in 1912, in regard to the committee's effort, that "the rural and small-town schools stand about where they were at the beginning of the agitation for improvement, except in certain areas in a few favored states" (pp. 12-13).

As industrialization continued its takeover of American society, the role of the schools remained under close scrutiny. With the recommendations of the Committee of Ten now twenty-five years old and seen as incongruous with the changing times, two significant events surfaced in 1918 that would alter the course that American curriculum would take: Franklin Bobbitt's book *The Curriculum* and the Cardinal Principles of Secondary Education, issued by the National Education Association under the direction of Clarence Kingsley. Kingsley, a math teacher in Brooklyn, gladly accepted the leadership role from the NEA, as he had long sought to amend what he felt was archaic thinking and practice in American education and the curriculum. Looking to reverse traditional social norms at every turn, he had completed his master's thesis with a study on homeless men, and at one point, exhibited a desire to work as a missionary in China (Kliebard, 1995b). The NEA group he spearheaded became known as the "Commission on the Reorganization of Secondary Education."

The increasingly diverse nation had some educators envisioning American schooling as becoming more of a socializing agent. It was felt by these educators that the content-driven curriculum of Harris, Eliot, the rest of the Committee of Ten and the other Humanists was not serving the needs of students, and that the situation would only worsen in ensuing decades. Rather, it was proposed that the secondary schools focus more on the training of citizenship and less of the academic rigor of Latin and Greek, and to a lesser degree, History, Geography, and Mathematics. The arrival of the Cardinal Principles on the curricular scene capped a quarter century of dissent on the subject-driven objectives of the Committee of Ten. Rather than focusing the curriculum on the traditional content areas, the Cardinal Principles called on American secondary schools to hone the skills of students in seven general "personal development" areas: Health, Command of Fundamental Processes, Worthy Home Membership, Vocation, Leisure Pursuits, Citizenship, and Ethical Character. This watershed event in American curriculum cannot be underestimated; for directly attributable to the Cardinal Principles, and as stated by Mirel and Angus (1994), the number of different types of courses offered in American high schools increased between 1922 and 1973 from about 175 to more than 2,100. At the same time, as noted by Kliebard (1995b), actual enrollment by high school students in this expanded array of courses steadily declined. Thus, the impact of the Cardinal Principles can be seen as the culmination of a gradual shift from the predominance of the traditional subject areas.

Roots of the Cardinal Principles' spirit were seen a few years earlier, and was noticed by Cubberly (1912). "The past ten to fifteen years have seen a marked change in the conception of school itself. The old information conception, with a curriculum limited closely to the old staple common-school subjects, is giving place to a new social, vocational, and economic conception of the school" (pp. 14-15). As Cubberly was primarily interested in the plight of rural schools, he saw a place for the agrarian sector in the new curriculum order. Many educators on the national scene believed that, despite getting word of the Cardinal Principles, most schools in rural areas would not be overly zealous to include them in the curriculum. Lessons learned from the Committee of Twelve suggested that rural schools would choose to forge their own destinies, with the input from the national level taken as extremely casual advice.

Bobbitt, called by some the "Father of Curriculum Studies" because of his first work (*The Curriculum* – followed by a second book that would appear in 1920 entitled *How to Make a Curriculum*), first became prominent through his association with a group of curriculum reformers known as the "Social Efficiency" educators (Kliebard, 1995a). Bolstered by the influential words of Frederick Taylor in his industrial manifesto *The Principles of Scientific Management*, the Social Efficiency group (also aided by the efforts of prominent curriculum reformers W.W. Charters and David Snedden) sought to apply the reason and operation of the manufacturing world to that of public schooling. Through a scientific study of society, it was believed, one could decipher the proper objectives that the school should attain and thus eliminate perceived "waste" that had existed in the curriculum. In turn, these objectives could also be revealed (and taught) to the masses in schools also through the scientific process – which later surfaced as the general origins of behaviorism. The tenets of the Social Efficiency educators are best presented by Bobbitt (1918, as quoted in Kliebard, 1995a):

> The central theory is simple. Human life, however varied, consists in the performance of specific activities. Education that prepares for life is one that prepares definitely and adequately for these specific activities. However numerous and diverse they may be for any social class, they can be discovered. This requires only that one go out into the world of affairs and discover the particular of which these affairs consist. These will show the abilities, attitudes, habits, appreciations, and forms of knowledge that men need. These will be the objectives of

the curriculum. They will be numerous, definite, and particularized. The curriculum will then be that series of experiences that children and youth must have by way of attaining those objectives. (p. 42)

The strongest ally of Bobbitt in the private sector quickly became Taylor. Carefully studying the various aspects of industry, Taylor wished to see everything directed towards precise efficiency. As Kliebard (1975) noted, "One of Taylor's proudest accomplishments was to inveigle a man he called Schmidt into increasing his handling of pig iron at a Bethlehem steel plant from twelve-and-a-half tons a day to forty-seven" (p. 53). And like Taylor, Bobbitt saw shame in the wastefulness of schools, particularly related to time spent on task. As he toured the Gary, Indiana schools in 1912, he witnessed his perceived waste firsthand. He likened the school to an industrial plant (and liberally referred to schools as "plants" in his reports), and "'The first principle of scientific management,' he announced, 'is to use all the plant all the available time'... He mourned the closing of the school plant in the summer, 'a loss of some 16 percent, no small item in the calculations of the efficiency engineer'" (ibid., p. 55). Bobbitt believed in a curriculum that was wide and expansive, yet carrying the most minute details of what was important to be learned in order to function in society. He also believed that the curriculum makers must not only be flexible enough to embrace change, but actually *foresee* change. "We must particularize the objectives of education," Bobbitt (1920b) claimed. "We, too, must institutionalize foresight, and, so far as the conditions of work will permit, develop a technique of predetermination of the particularized results to be aimed at" (p. 738). As a counterpoint to Bobbitt in his day, John Dewey (1922) was careful to make clear that child interests should not dominate selections for the curriculum; rather, they should simply add to them. He notes that "men do not shoot because targets exist, but they set up targets in order that throwing and shooting may be more effective and significant" (p. 226).

The frustration of nearly all the groups calling for curriculum reform – from the Herbartians to the Social Efficiency educators, and all camps in between – was summarized in the historic Twenty-sixth yearbook of the National Society for the Study of

Education, published in 1926. It was, as characterized by Schubert (1980), "A monumental effort by curriculum scholars from many persuasions to produce a unified statement" (p. 66). None of the reform groups – either separately or together – had been able to fully supplant the traditional, Humanist curriculum affirmed by the Committee of Ten thirty-three years earlier. Therefore, the volume mostly turned out to be a compilation of frustration, a sum of failed efforts lasting a third of a century.

An aging Charles Eliot, in his late eighties when the Social Efficiency educators were enjoying the pinnacle of their success, cautioned the public in the previous decade (1908) to be wary of the increased production sought of the standardized movements of the worker under Taylor's principles; that there was an inherent danger in embracing such a system on a widespread scale. "The inevitable result," Eliot said of the would-be scrutinized worker, "was the destruction of the interest of the workman in his work." Nonetheless, as industry grew in the 1920s, the movement for Social Efficiency doctrine gained momentum in the schools as well. The idea of "factory model" production of school graduates seemed to make sense and be in coordination with a newly-mechanized society. In the midst of the prosperity of the decade, however, some forward-thinking educators saw storm clouds on the horizon. It was imagined by some that the massive disparity of wealth would ultimately catch up with the nation. So when the stock market crashed in October of 1929, a landmark prelude to the Great Depression that followed, many things associated with a capitalistic society were called into question – including the curriculum being taught in schools. Thus brought to the fore was yet another curricular reform group, known as the "Reconstructionists." With the United States and the rest of the world suffering through the height of the Depression in 1932, a man by the name of George Counts addressed the annual meeting of the Progressive Education Association with a speech entitled "Dare the School Build a New Social Order?" Within his words, Counts (1932) condemned the state of American education, but said that the time is ripe for change. "The age is pregnant with possibilities... like all peoples, Americans have a sublime faith in education," he claimed. Counts also decried the very structure of the PEA – an outfit which, in the eyes of Counts, had become a loosely-coordinated and ill-defined organization which had not accomplished any substantive "progress" in school operation. Counts conceded that they were good at causing a ruckus, but little else to that point. "Like a baby shaking a rattle," he said of the minimal results of the PEA bantering, "we seem to be utterly content with action, providing is noisy enough." For true reform, Counts asserted, teachers and students in American schools needed to be willing change agents. And to be effective change agents, they must address what Counts called the ten fallacies of a society based on what he viewed as capitalistic flaw. As an example, he continues in his speech, "There is the fallacy that man is born free. He is not born free. Rather, he pursues freedom through the avenues of culture."

While often mistaken as a "child-centered" curricular philosophy, the Reconstructionists concerned themselves more with the envisioned future society as the new curriculum is planned – a society based on social and economic justice (Brameld, 1971). Reconstructionists were the short-term descendants of the Social Meliorist reform group, one of the camps that attempted to overthrow the Humanists after the Committee of Ten's proclamations. To the Reconstructionist, the prevailing question remained, "Education for what?" – meaning, "For what social purpose is each aspect of the curriculum intended?"

Impacting curriculum on the rural scene the most with the advent of the Depression was not the Reconstructionist platform, but rather the continued storm of school consolidation. It remained a looming destiny for most small rural schools into the 1930s, as noted by Fuller (1994). "Between 1926 and 1934, the number of consolidations nationwide had increased by 27 percent. By 1933-34, there had been more than 17,000 consolidated schools in the continental United States" (pp. 107-108).

A colleague of Counts from Columbia Teachers' College in New York (and fellow Reconstructionist) was Harold Rugg, who commenced the final major curricular audit before the United States' entrance into World War Two – "The Eight-Year Study" (1932-1940). As divided as the progressive education movement appeared to be to Counts, by 1932 it yet coalesced enough power to impose a longitudinal challenge on the traditional curriculum. In the midst of their movement, the Reconstructionists attempted to free the students from the alleged confinements of the traditional, humanities-based curriculum that had been affirmed by the Committee of Ten. They contended that the main culprit in maintaining the status quo was the higher education system, as noted by Kliebard (1995a). "By the early

1930s, the conviction became firmly implanted in the minds of curriculum reformers that the colleges were the principal impediment to curriculum reform at the secondary school level" (p. 183). Chamberlin and his associates (1942), contemporaries of the Reconstructionists, added that "the prescription by the colleges, either directly or indirectly, as to what courses the secondary schools must teach, reflects a fundamental distrust between the two educational levels" (p. 211). In 1930, Rugg had formed within the ranks of the PEA the Commission on the Relation of School and College. The commission sought to explore possibilities for curricular experimentation, but feared a backlash against students engaged in such curricula when the students applied for college. Finally, however, their request was granted. In September, 1933, after three years of planning, thirty schools took part in an unprecedented experiment in the American secondary school curriculum through the lobbying of the PEA. The experiment offered these schools the flexibility to infuse new curricula into the school setting, curricula that would be based more on student choice and non-traditional subject matter than ever before. Colleges and universities agreed to accept the performance of students (provided that it was of quality) as worthy criteria for admission for the duration of the study. The experiment's eight years were designed to track the students' progress through their four years of high school, their four years of college, and then to follow up on the graduates' first year in the workforce afterwards. One school would eventually remove itself, leaving the sample number at twenty-nine. As Kliebard (1995a) pointed out, however, the sample may have been invalid from the outset. "Schools had to demonstrate their willingness to experiment with their curricula to be eligible, and this tended to skew the sample strongly toward the prestigious private schools whose headmasters still constituted a significant element in the Progressive Education Association" (p. 184).

The schools spent the first two years of the program (academic years 1932-33 and 1933-34) implementing whatever changes in the curriculum they saw fit; basically, no restrictions or limitations were placed on their revisions. "The Thirty Schools differed widely as to the extent to which they experimented," Chamberlin, et al. (1942) revealed. Some eliminated Latin, a staple of the American curriculum since the reaffirmation of the 1828 Yale Faculty Report by the Committee of Ten; other schools introduced new literature to their language programs; still others integrated greater helpings of the industrial and mechanical arts. As noted by Schubert (1980), however, part of this variety became a problem. "Little programmatic similarity existed among the experimental schools; experiences had by experimental students were quite diverse, making it difficult to generalize about the best curriculum organization or pattern developed" (p. 102).

The results of the entire Eight-Year Study were published in 1942 in a five-volume set. A total of 2,108 graduates from the 29 schools were followed through their collegiate years, although it should be noted that 1,475 of the graduates were paired "against" a similar graduate from a traditionally-prepared program.

According to Chamberlin, et al. (1942), the general findings about the experiential graduates from the Eight-Year Study found that they, in comparison to the traditionally-prepared students:

- Earned a slightly higher total grade average

- Earned higher grade averages in all subject fields except foreign language

- Specialized in the same academic fields as the comparison students

- Did not differ from the comparison students in the number of times they were placed on probation

- Received slightly more academic honors each year

- Were more often judged to possess a high degree of intellectual curiosity and drive

- Were more often judged to by systematic, precise, and objective in their thinking

- Were more often judged to have developed clear or well-formulated ideas concerning the meaning of education – especially in the first two years of college

- More often demonstrated a high degree of resourcefulness in meeting new situations

- Did not differ from the comparison group in ability to plan their time effectively

- Had about the same problems of adjustment as the comparison group, but approached their solution with greater effectiveness

- Participated somewhat more frequently, and more often enjoyed appreciative experiences, in the arts

- Participated more in all organized student groups except religious and "service" activities

- Earned in each college year a higher percentage of non-academic honors

- Did not differ from comparison group in the quality of adjustment to their contemporaries

- Differed only slightly from the comparison group in the kinds of judgments about their schooling

- Had a somewhat better orientation toward the choice of a vocation

- Demonstrated a more active concern for what was going on in the world (pp. 207-208)

In a concluding statement, Chamberlin, et al. (1942) pronounced the overall results as a resounding victory for progressive curricula against the traditional form. "It is quite obvious from these data that the Thirty Schools graduates, as a group, have done a somewhat better job than the comparison group whether success is judged by college standards, by the students' contemporaries, or by the individual students" (p. 208). Others, however, viewed the long comparison as nothing more than a stalemate – and thus a victory for the traditional curriculum, which the progressive curriculum failed to supplant; in other words, the challenger and the champion fought to a draw, so the champion retained his title.

In reference to the effort by the thirty schools, Kliebard (1975) claimed there was, and perhaps continues to be, something almost "spiritual" in the job of the curriculum theorizer. "The major research in the field, such as the Eight-Year Study, are basically efforts to establish the primacy of the forces of good over the forces of wickedness and reaction" (p. 42). Such sentiment was also seen in the beliefs of Harris, as the carefully-laid, time-honored curriculum is what allows the student to "know himself" and connect with his heritage.

Due in part to notoriety gained from spearheading the Eight-Year Study, Rugg enjoyed considerable success with his concurrent series of Social Studies textbooks which offered, in his view, a more holistic view of civic and historical training. The "Frontier" series, as it was called, enjoyed popularity through the 1930s but sales had dimmed by 1941, and most school districts had discontinued requests for it. The downfall of series was cemented when patriotic groups such as the American Legion and the Veterans of Foreign Wars denounced the texts as "anti-American," and Counts, Rugg, and other Reconstructionists were soon investigated by the Central Intelligence Agency as possible communists.

While Bobbitt was working at the University of Chicago in the 1920s, a young graduate student by the name of Ralph Tyler was already entering the curriculum debate from the behaviorist perspective. By the 1940s, Tyler had established his own reputation as a scholar, as he produced his historic *Basic Principles of Curriculum and Instruction*, a framework for curriculum making that is followed (to varying degrees) to this day. This framework, which came to be known as "The Tyler Rationale," launched a new era in behaviorist theory in learning. Tyler stressed that it was what the *student* did in the classroom – not the teacher – that was important. Through his four-step procedure of creating and exercising curriculum (the formulation of objectives, the formulation of learning experiences, the organization of the learning experiences, and evaluation of the process), a change in behavior was to be seen in the student; in other words, there was to be a skill present afterwards that was not present beforehand.

In the selection of objectives, Tyler (1949) made it clear that no single source should suffice; not only subject area specialists, but also philosophy, life outside the school, and the students themselves can all contribute, among others. These objectives (which Tyler actually called "purposes") were carefully deliberated and selected, in the spirit of Bobbitt and his social efficiency doctrine. Learning experiences would be then meticulously selected and organized so that, together, they would provide for students the "greatest cumulative effect" (p. 103). Finally, students and teachers would reflect on the learning process to determine if the desired learning (i.e., change in behavior) took place.

Summary

By 1918, the gradual pressure on the Committee of Ten's Humanist curriculum culminated in the publication of the Cardinal Principles of Secondary Education, formulated through the National Education Association under the direction of Brooklyn math teacher Clarence Kingsley. This document signified a gradual, 25-year shift in focus in the American curriculum from traditional subjects to personal skills. While the time-honored subjects remained in the curriculum (and certainly, still comprise a majority of it), it was then believed that they should be transmitted to students in a more practical light, in a manner that would serve the civic needs of the growing society. The Cardinal Principles emerged at time when one of the maverick curricular groups, the Social Efficiency educators, were gaining popularity with their methodologies that paralleled the booming industrial economy.

As with the recommendations of the Committee of Ten, the dictum of the Cardinal Principles was received by rural schools, but loosely followed due to differing local need. Prominent national educators once again experienced the difficulty in trying to nationalize rural schools, as oversight was nearly impossible for all the outlying schoolhouses across the land. As the United States entered the Great Depression, however, the national scene shifted once again, as all curriculum – urban, rural, and otherwise – came under scrutiny by a few radical groups, as did the principles of capitalism and the distribution of wealth.

After victory in World War Two, servicemen and women returned to civilian life with new educational opportunities through the Servicemen's Readjustment Act (commonly known as the G.I. Bill). This act allowed many to return the classroom and finish school, where a new behaviorist mode, originally born out of the Social Efficiency Educators, was leading the curriculum charge behind the flag of Ralph Tyler of the University of Chicago. The provision for selecting objectives in the "Tyler Rationale" would remain a constant in the nation's schools for the remainder of the century.

5. Conant's Consolidation Push and the Modern Era of Rural Curriculum, 1951-2003

> Behold the turtle. He makes progress only when he sticks his neck out.
>
> – James Conant

By the 1950s, most of the smoke had cleared from the first national blast of rural school consolidation as ordered by the Committee of Twelve in 1897, as well as from the first wide-scale battle for control of the American curriculum – a battle that had lasted sixty years. In the end, the subject-dominated curriculum of Harris and the Humanists prevailed, for no greater reason than simple resistance to change in the structures of American education. The concession that systemic change was improbable was acknowledged by nearly everyone. "Even John Dewey," Kliebard (1998) wrote, "the quintessential American educational reformer, was, more often than not, interested in reconstructing the existing subjects than replacing them with something else" (p. 32). In addition, it was clear that programs from the Eight-Year Study in itself had not succeeded in supplanting the traditional curriculum, as noted by Schubert (1980). "Despite the results of the Eight-Year Study, the curriculum pendulum in the early Fifties swung away from the experientialists" (p. 175). And the recommendations stated in the Cardinal Principles of 1918 did diversify the American curriculum, and for a time took attention away from the traditional subjects. For the most part, however, this was only fleeting, as we see grammar, literature, history, and mathematics continuing to dominate today – with a strong case still being made for these subjects, of course – along with a relatively slight inclusion of science and technology.

Perhaps it was simply a matter of convenience that the curriculum remained generally the same into the second half of the twentieth century, as Kliebard (1998) continues:

> At the same time that some proponents of curriculum reform were proclaiming that the curriculum should be derived from the spontaneous interests of children, others were claiming that the curriculum should be a direct and specific preparation for adulthood. Still others saw an urgent need to infuse into the curriculum a strong element of social criticism. Each doctrine had an appeal and a constituency. And rather than make a particular ideological choice among apparently contradictory curriculum directions, it was perhaps more politically expedient on the part of practical school administrators to make a potpourri of all of them. This, in fact, is what the American curriculum has become. (Ibid.)

With their opponents perhaps weary from a long, drawn-out fight lasting several decades, the traditionalists in the curriculum field reclaimed a certain amount of territory in the 1950s. The anti-establishment groups, ranging from the Social Efficiency educators of the 1920s through Counts and Reconstructionists of the 1930s and beyond, were not convincing in their displacement of the Humanist position (see Counts, 1952). Instead, the rogue, maverick reputation of the alternative theories was always a cause for skepticism, as noted further by Schubert (1980). "Although progressivism was manifest in the literature from 1920 to the mid-1940s, it always embodied an experientialist curriculum that took a back seat to the intellectual traditionalists in practice" (p. 175).

Despite fighting to a general stalemate for three years in the Korean War, the United States was still cruising along in an era of post-World War Two euphoria into the mid-1950s. And notwithstanding military buildups by the Soviet Union, the U.S. – both militarily and in general science – remained on the technological cutting edge. However, the nation was caught off guard when the Soviets launched the satellite *Sputnik* into orbit in 1957, the first of its kind in the world. It was viewed as a watershed moment in technological advancement, and one for worry on the part of the United States. Not in a hundred years had a nation so grandly catapulted above America in scientific ingenuity, and an immediate blaming finger was pointed at the public education system – and in particular, the "softness" of the curriculum (a theme that would later resound through the reports of the National Commission for Excellence in Education, the 1983 group behind the scalding "A Nation at Risk" document). In response to what was perceived a veritable encroachment on American exclusivity in the Space Race, the United States Congress passed a bill in 1958 later entitled the "National Defense Education Act" – a phrase that in itself implied a militaristic position. The act called for more stringent training in mathematics and the sciences, as well as the spread of foreign language instruction and the identification of more gifted students (and, consequently, pushing these students into the sciences). As if announcing a civil crisis, the act (known also as Public Law 85-864) stated that everyone had a role in the job to be done. "The Congress hereby finds and declares that the security of the Nation requires the fullest development of the mental resources and technical skills of its young men and women... to meet the present educational emergency requires additional effort at all levels of government" (p. 473). As was seen before this time, and has been seen afterwards, *fear* became the main propeller of curriculum change in American schools. But fear as an agent for curriculum change had not been heard from for the last time in the 1950s; later, it would be revisited in the debate over the acceptable size of a school and its curriculum.

As the National Defense Education Act took its influence into the various depths of the education establishment, new theory was especially sought on the teaching of science. Among the most prominent movements in this realm came from noted psychologist Jerome Bruner and his idea of a "spiraled curriculum" (Willis, et al., 1994). Bruner wanted to uncover the common attributes which lay in all human minds, and harness this power to unlock problem-solving capabilities yet to be seen. To do this, he proposed, it was necessary to exercise better control over the curriculum; that is, not to have infinite numbers of unconnected concepts, but to rely on a few important concepts to be revisited and further developed throughout a student's scholastic career. In this way, Bruner proposed, timeless knowledge could be used as a strong basis for engaging a flexible, changeable curriculum in the future – particularly, in the sciences and technology.

Improvements in transportation throughout the 1930s, '40s, and '50s had strengthened the argument for continued consolidation of rural schools. With better automobiles, the long-standing impediment of bringing children to school from a long distance appeared to be dissipating by the 1950s. The Committee of Twelve had called for the improvement of roads for this purpose, although the means of transportation were yet limited at the time of its report in 1897. Even more influential than improved transportation, however, were compelling arguments for the elimination of the small school brought by James B. Conant during the late 1950s and early '60s. Conant served in numerous diplomatic and educational capacities on the national and international scene, and pushed (1959, 1963) the idea of the "comprehensive" American high school to provide the rural student (and all students) with a greater variety of curricular opportunities. The small rural high school, in his view, was incapable of affording the instruction necessary for modern society.

> The prevalence of such high schools – those with graduating classes of less than 100 students – constitutes one of the serious obstacles to good secondary education throughout most of the United States. I believe that such schools are not in a position to provide a satisfactory education for any group of their students... A small high school cannot by its very nature offer a comprehensive curriculum. (p. 77)

Interestingly, a substantial number of the so-called "unsatisfactory" schools remained in the United States into the 1990s, as cited precisely by Nachtigal (1992) – those with graduating classes of 100 or fewer, as proclaimed by Conant. "In the upper Midwest, for example, as high as 83% of the secondary schools would fall below the 100 students per grade level that conventional wisdom suggests is necessary to provide a comprehensive educational program" (p. 74). Thus, fear again – this time, fear of a curriculum that could not compete with larger schools – became a force for change.

Although surely a local issue, Conant (1967) later stressed that the "elimination" of the small high school must also be closely supervised at the state level (p. 82). He pointed to New York and California as excellent examples of effective consolidation, where "imaginative leadership, shrewd political thinking, and a willingness to offer 'an alluring carrot' [state subsidies to consolidated areas] have been effective in promoting school district reorganization" (p. 84). He also made a stern, ominous warning to those states unwilling to cooperate with his strategy. "In other states, less informed interests dominate," he asserted. "High schools remain small. These states just cannot make their proper contributions to the national effort. If citizens in these states face up to the implications of their failure to act, action may be forthcoming" (pp. 84-85). So, as was seen in the Committee of Twelve, it appeared that rural citizens unwilling to face the changes of consolidation would have change thrust upon them regardless.

In 1961, Conant was also commissioned by the Carnegie Corporation to conduct a study of the state of teacher education in the U.S. While admitting that he could not visit all 50 states, Conant concentrated his study on teacher education programs in the 16 most populous states at the time. These included California, Florida, Georgia, Illinois, Indiana, Massachusetts, Michigan, Missouri, New Jersey, New York, North Carolina, Ohio, Pennsylvania, Virginia, Texas, and Wisconsin. In this study as well – although not directly related to the issue of consolidation – he framed his arguments for improved teacher preparation around the structure of academic systems that were complete with large schools with expansive curricula. He believed that a teacher could operate effectively only in an environment that was intellectually enriching; and he expressed, both implicitly and explicitly, that such an environment was not available in certain small rural schools that continued to operate.

Therefore, with Conant's influential leadership, the conventional wisdom of "bigger being better" continued. The comprehensive high school was finding its way out of the city and was beginning to impact the simple, one-room schoolhouses found in isolated rural areas. Standing as a firm, unwavering institution in education, consolidation continued to literally re-shape the rural school landscape into the 1960s.

The reports made by Conant did indeed greatly impact the content to be offered in American high schools. By the late 1960s and early 1970s, however, other scholars had witnessed the replacement of "content" with "form" as the basis of curriculum, and thus a type of "retreat" by teachers into a relative role of obscurity in curriculum-making. Goodlad (1969) identified a particular rift between educational research and curriculum development. "If the abstract categories of research and discourse bear no identifiable relationship to the existing phenomena called curricula," he stated, "then there is, indeed, cause for concern" (p. 369). Bussis, et al. (1976) also noted that "over the years, educational research has basically sapped curriculum of its content meaning and injected in its place a 'methods' or 'forms' emphasis. This metamorphosis has been achieved by the persisting preoccupation with questions about the formulation and use of educational objectives, the form and organization of curricular materials, and the methods of presenting material" (p. 10). Schaffarzich (1976) even claimed that the question of *who had control* over curriculum decision-making was taking precedence over content, as the process became paramount. This process, however, was viewed by some as becoming an activity without regard for its own past, as described by Davis (1977). "The curriculum field is a largely activist, non-reflective enterprise," he stated. "Forward is the generally perceived direction of movement" (p. 159). In other words, the mindset of some educators of the 1960s and '70s was that the "past lives" of curriculum development theories are something to be escaped and not embraced for any value.

Different instructional movements also took place in the 1960s and early '70s that impacted curriculum development as well. A group labeling themselves as the "Radical School Reformers" sought to "free" the student from the "evil, tyrannical"triumvirate of the teacher, school, and curriculum. As was the scene in other social arenas of the day, those in power in the schools were viewed by the Radical Reformers as nothing short of "jailers," whose overreaching authority not only kept students physically captive but intellectually as well. Needless to say, the group also had little use for the traditional curriculum, calling instead for what they deemed the

"Relevant Curriculum," one devised per individual student interest or need and vacant of any prescription on part of the Establishment. However, as has been seen in recent protests at political conventions, outsiders to education had trouble ascertaining what exactly it was that the protesters were protesting. Ultimately, it was seen that the Radical School Reformers were a by-product of the 1960s, a group swept up in the emotional turbulence of the era and possessing little force for change.

In 1977, Ralph Tyler (at the age of 75) offered a reappraisal of the Tyler Rationale nearly thirty years after it had been originally presented. Its influence on curriculum-making continued to be profound – be it more out of nepotistic habit than anything else. By the 1970s it had been printed in more than a dozen languages, and its circulation continued to run in the thousands (Willis, et al., 1994). In retrospect, Tyler bemoaned how modern education had ignored the learner's "active role" in the curriculum-making process. "Human beings cannot be forced to learn intellectual and emotional behavior," he wrote. "Only under coercion or when offered tempting rewards will they even attempt a learning task which seems to them meaningless or distasteful" (p. 396). In light of the breakdown of traditional institutions in society, Tyler also viewed the job of the curriculum-maker in 1977 to be more important than ever before.

> It is (also) clear that there is a great erosion taking place in the total educational system in America. The home, the working place, the religious institutions, and the educational milieu of the community are furnishing fewer constructive learning experiences for young people than was true in the past. It is particularly necessary now in curriculum development to give careful consideration to the non-school areas of student learning. (p. 400)

It is reasonable to claim the most influential document affecting American curriculum in 1980s was *A Nation at Risk*, circulated widely by the NCEE in 1983. The commission was conceived to examine the efficacy of the American curriculum and school in light of recent economic competition, particularly from Japan and Germany. The report suggested that the curriculum had "softened," and that a refocusing on core subjects areas (a "back-to-basics" approach) was needed for American schools to become internationally competitive once again. Perhaps more importantly, it invited teachers to once again take an active role in the process of curriculum development. To this point, many contemporary rural school administrators had experienced frustration in being alone in designing the curriculum for their schools; *A Nation at Risk* called on all teachers – in rural, urban, and suburban settings – to consider it a part of their professional responsibility to take part in this process, and to not leave curricular decisions solely to the principal or superintendent under whom they worked.

Primarily, the report focused on its call for a longer school year (as was the case, comparatively, in Germany and Japan), up to 200 or even 220 days; the involvement and responsibility of parents and students as well as teachers in the reform process; and concentration on what was called the "New Basics" – for all intents and purposes, a recitation of Harris's Five Windows to the Soul, with computer/technology training included as well. As recounted by Bennett (1992), the spirit of the report was its address of what had become the corruption of the contemporary curriculum since the 1960s. "English, history, math, and science gave way to a curriculum lacking substance, coherence, or consistent structure [in the '60s]; it was replaced by faddish, trivial, and intellectually shallow courses" (p. 53).

It was indeed a wake-up call. The authors referred to the dilution of the American curriculum as nothing less than "educational disarmament." Statements like these reminded citizens that the Cold War was most certainly alive and well in the early 1980s, and it reminded old-time educators of the militaristic stance resulting from the National Defense Education Act of 1958. For, as *A Nation at Risk* glumly pointed out, "We have even squandered the gains in achievement made in the wake of the Sputnik challenge" (p. 1).

As the Twentieth Century came to a close, the curriculum field found itself yet in the midst of what has been termed the "Post-Modern" era. Modernism, with its reliance on the scientific process for answers to all things, had lost favor with most of academia as a multitude of aesthetic, alternative viewpoints began to dominate the curriculum. It has been the position of the Post-Modernists that not all things in life (let alone in the curriculum) fit neatly into the scientific, calculative box; that there is always room for open interpretation, even in matters of formulaic inquiry.

Summary

As was the case in the first half of the 1900s, the curriculum of American schools in the second half of the century was dominated by the given priorities of the decade or era. Technology challenges from the Soviets, the Civil Rights movement, economic advancements by Germany and Japan, and a host of other events dictated the subjects studied in classrooms. Herbert Kliebard, whose wrap-up of the curriculum debate in 1900 announced an "untidy compromise" among competing parties, might have issued the same summary in the year 2000. He (1975) proclaimed a forecast of the duty of the next generation of curriculum-makers. "The next fifty years in the curriculum field is essentially one of developing alternatives to the mode of thinking and the limited framework that has so clearly dominated our first fifty years" (p. 49). Now, after the turn of another century and more than halfway to Kliebard's landmark, the complexity of society might suggest that the job of the curriculum-maker is even more difficult than could ever have been imagined.

6. Politics and Curriculum Development in the Modern Rural School

Politics in education are vicious precisely because the political stakes are so small.

– Henry Kissinger

As seen, the small rural school has been caught in the crossfire of curriculum debates since the meeting of the Committee of Ten in 1893. Reform was first sought for schools in urban areas when change was needed, and it was expected that "weaker" schools in rural America would simply follow suit. As the United States heads into the twenty-first century, new forms of political empowerment are needed for rural areas to protect their rightful voices in the process of educational reform; however, those in place need to be maintained and observed as well. In the 2000 presidential election, Democratic Party nominee Al Gore received more popular votes than Texas Governor and Republican Party nominee George W. Bush, but Governor Bush won the election with more electoral votes. This caused Gore supporters to call for reform of the system, with some wishing to go to an election format that follows popular vote only. However, the very purpose for which the electoral system was implemented in the early days of our nation still serves its duty today. While Gore supporters claimed that the electoral system denied individuals a voice with decisions made by a select few, the actual reason for the electoral system was – and is – to protect the vote of the isolated rural citizenry against the more densely-conglomerated urban areas of the country. If the electoral college was to go by the wayside, a dramatic and unjust shift of voter power would go to more populated regions. The Electoral College stands as one example of policy that most knowledgeable rural citizens would find worth preserving.

Furthermore, while there are a number of outside variables working on the civic empowerment of rural areas (both positively and negatively), there is also a wide range of political forces involved in the rural sector – and in many cases, particular to the rural sector. Among the most prominent of these variables is the simple ability to communicate among citizens, school officials, and bureaucrats. Difficulties with communication descend into teaching platoons as well.

Despite diminutive size and personnel numbers, small rural schools may not always have effective communication operations; the fact that a school is "small" – either indigenously or through a de-centralization campaign – will not guarantee that quality communication takes place among its staff. Communication, like any product of human existence, must come from within the teachers themselves. An atmosphere of open communication is not conferred from on high, but it is rather developed through the persistent efforts of individuals, who value its role in the long-term success of an organization. In other words, although good communication can be encouraged, it cannot be coerced; the people involved must desire to have it. Furthermore, when one considers the history of rural school curriculum (as examined previously), it is evident that all rural schools and rural areas do not possess the same culture; educational policy and strategies must be interpretable locally in order to be effective. This phenomenon is not unique to K-12 schooling, as the small rural school has been typically disconnected from the curricular resources of higher education as well (Schmidt, et al., 1994; Moriarity, 1981).

With a school board-approved curriculum or other structured learning system in force, the surrounding community often has a large impact on what is taught in the small rural high school. Prospects for curricular change may be less a matter of faculty discussion, and reflect more of a "town consensus." Furthermore, a small school system may not even choose to hire a teacher or school administrator who will not perpetuate the local value system (Peshkin, 1978). The local school board is often comprised of individuals who may represent the "old guard" in a given town and who seek to promulgate the status quo in terms of school employees. Thus, it is important to investigate the nature of rural school-community interaction in the United States and the resulting impact of the local community upon curricular reform efforts undertaken by a school staff.

Until the advent of industrialization and urbanization in the late nineteenth century, the strong bond of community and togetherness within the United States was found in rural settings. Nachtigal and Theobald (1995) discussed the "culture" of being part of a rural community and the seemingly-endangered situations that this culture is currently experiencing. The authors noted that the phrase "bigger is better" continues to serve as the conventional wisdom for schools, as was furthered before the end of the progressive era (p. 132). This "wisdom" is fueled, they state, by the proportional growth of other facets of American life. As cities, factories, and businesses have grown larger and larger with each passing decade, the conventional wisdom tells citizens that schools must continue to expand in size as well, a position made in no uncertain terms by Conant. The authors pointed out that despite not having a significant research base to continue this orientation to size, Americans "cling to it as some kind of basic truth" (p. 133).

Furthermore, Sher (1995) wrote that "virtually all [educational] reformers – from the religious right to the secular progressives – loathe the industrial/factory model of schooling that has come to dominate American K-12 education" (p. 143). How, then, does a small rural school district re-assert its autonomy and strength in the midst of an amalgamated world? Tyree (1996) claimed that 60% of U.S. school districts are in the rural sector and that it is necessary for the academic community at-large to "understand the diverse needs and provide support, emotional and physical, for these rural families" (p. 15).

In terms of viewing the future curriculum of rural schools (and preventing the continuous erosion of the agrarian educational landscape), Nachtigal and Theobald (1995) present three objectives for educators:

> - Any re-formulation of schools should bear in mind the focus of creating viable rural communities, which will be an organic, revolving process;
>
> - Any re-formulation of schools in viable rural communities must hold a dual set of expectations – one set in keeping with an expanded mission for the school and one set concerning how the process of schooling takes place; and
>
> - Enhancing the viable rural community must entail more than simply creating more jobs – it must include a re-discovered appreciation of the history, art, literature, and music of the region. (p. 135)

Thus, strengthening the small rural community may be directly linked to the revitalization of its schools, so long as a new awareness of the cultural surroundings (as well as the practical needs) of the area is forged. This idea supported by Wall, et al. (1991), who envisioned five themes as setting the tone for students to become productive "entrepreneurs" in building strong rural communities:

> - Classroom teachers who are people of energy, vision, and commitment;
>
> - Careful planning for school and community growth;
>
> - Enterprises undertaken that fit into a niche in the community economy;
>
> - A school curriculum that emphasizes strengthening students' entrepreneurial skills; and
>
> - A school that works closely with the community, on a consistent basis. (p. 18)

The formation of the curriculum and other operations for the small town school, therefore, can become a matter of extensive community discussion, painstaking budget reduction, and careful determination of local needs in the view of many commentators on the scene. The process of developing an adequate curriculum with limited funds is indeed a challenge. Lack of funding, however, is only one of many hurdles that educators and townspeople encounter when attempting to improve their schools. Queitzsch and Nelson (1996) identified some of the major issues of rural school reform, as they sampled teachers in 120 agrarian districts in Oregon, Washington, Idaho, Montana, and Alaska. When presented with twenty scholastic issues in regard to school reform, the informants decided if each issue was a priority to curricular reform, as noted below:

Curricular Reform Priorities

Item	
Strengthening instructional strategies (such as critical thinking and cooperative learning) to improve student achievement	83.2
Aligning assessment with *curriculum* and instruction	81.5
Integrating curriculum across subjects and levels	79.0
Preparing students for the 21st century global marketplace	70.6
Incorporating and meeting state standards and requirements	67.2
Identifying desired learner outcomes and performance goals	67.2
Developing and implementing a process for renewing and restructuring the *curriculum*	66.4
Developing alternative assessments that are performance-based and authentic	66.4

In addition, the informants were asked to identify constraints to implementing these reforms in their areas. Twenty-two percent cited "insufficient time" as the main obstacle – time that was limited due to multiple class preparations and non-instructional duties before and after school unique to their rural school settings, due to a lack of personnel or other reasons. Eighteen percent noted "insufficient funding" as the chief deterrent, fourteen percent claimed "insufficient expertise," thirteen percent "insufficient personnel," and seven percent "insufficient technology." Other factors included: Lack of consensus in school (7.6%) and community (5.1%); no opportunity to join a network (2.2%) or consortium (1.9%); and finally, problems with community isolation (5.7%), disinterest (2.8%), and partnerships (0.9%) (p. 19), indicating there were a variety of agendas in the minds of these small-school educators. To be successful, it is evident that all stakeholders in the school (teachers, parents, administrators, and townspeople) must take active roles in the reform process, and often it is ultimately left up to the principals in the individual school buildings to remove the final barriers to reform, such as those listed above (see also Manges & Wilcox, 1997).

The local school board is indeed an interesting arena in which the small town often demonstrates unique curricular discourse, with the values of the community coming to the fore as they are locally established (Peshkin, 1978; Theobald, 1995). Peshkin (1978) noted the unified attitude of the board members on issues that directly affected the curriculum of the schools in "Mansfield." This was particularly true in the case of Bert Holcomb, George Robinson, and Rex Borden, who grew up in Mansfield, were products of the school system, and shared an unwavering concern for the community that one might expect from indigenous citizens.

> Holcomb, Robinson, and Borden share a common way of life as native Mansfielders and alumni of Mansfield High School; they have been shaped by the same powerful experiences. Faced with the task of maintaining the Mansfield school system, they respond in similar ways. Discord is absent from board meetings; few motions fail to get a unanimous vote. Though differentiated by age, temperament, and interests, board members clearly converge on matters involving school and community. (p. 66)

It is apparent in Peshkin's study that the school board members were emotionally vested in the town of Mansfield; the decisions they make are of direct consequence to each and every citizen of the community, and the values they convey are, perhaps, a true representation of Mansfield's philosophy of education. Further, it is noted that the board members pursue employees (teachers, administrators, and even cooks) that ascribe to the local ideal. For example, they are not interested in hiring a superintendent who checks his watch repeatedly (as one unsuccessful candidate did throughout his interview!), but rather works until a job is done – much like a job that is done on the farm. In terms of the board members themselves, Peshkin noted that only the "right candidates" are elected by the residents of Mansfield. "The right candidates are those without the kind of axes to grind which might disrupt the status quo" (p. 60). Thus, it can be seen how the small town seeks to implant educational personnel who will strive to maintain the values that the community has set forth. This tradition of local interpretation might be traced back to the one-room schoolhouse, as illustrated by Leight and Rinehart (1992):

> Life in the rural school tended to be a reflection of the rural lifestyle. For example, although they began and ended at specific times, the schedule *within* the school day was relatively flexible. There were none of the bells or buzzers that cut into lessons in today's school, signaling that it is time to "turn off" reading and "turn on" mathematics. (p. 137)

In looking at Peshkin's example, fostering dialogue between the leaders of a small-town school system and its residents can be problematic, particularly in discussing issues of curriculum (see also Bainer, 1997; Boone, 1998). Moriarity (1981) examined the perceptions of administrators in western South Dakota and how the rural nature of the area enhanced or detracted from community participation in curricular decisions. He found that 50% of the rural school leaders reported working directly with the community and the lack of appreciation for education as a "unique administrative challenge" (p. 2). The indifference these citizens held about the worth of formal schooling for their children propels this feeling. Involving the town in school-related policy is often a difficult task to engage. Furthermore, he found:

> Approximately 30% of the administrators identified curricular continuity, quality, and change as a major challenge. They are plagued with a shortage of relevant curricular materials, instructional equipment, and the technical know-how to use the resources they do have. The lack of any support system on a continuous basis from either the state or higher education provides them with little time for developing new curricular models. (p. 3)

School administrators in rural South Dakota plainly feel as isolated as their locales – isolated without finances, materials, or personnel for curricular change or improvement. Without the input of the community, the principal or superintendent is left to construct a solitary version of the educational policy for the area. While this scenario may appeal to an autocratic type of school leader, it may not adequately represent the needs of all educational stakeholders under the person's jurisdiction.

According to certain scholars, the construction and maintenance of the rural curriculum will often encounter two significant barriers: the traditional tendencies of general school policy, and the traditional tendencies of the given community. Long ago, Bobbitt (1925) had noted that all early twentieth-century teachers were bound by the textbook-oriented, fact-dispersing methods of established schooling:

> Teachers have long been accustomed to thinking in terms of subjects, textbooks, recitations, examinations, etc., all of which belong to the older traditional conception. Most of our educational machinery tends to reinforce and maintain the traditional attitudes and valuations... only a few rare teachers, it appears, have achieved the necessary intellectual liberation. (p. 655)

The maintenance of traditional pedagogy seems to stem from an unchanging, obsolete curriculum; the very practices within the classroom serve to reinforce the curriculum in place, leaving it even more immobile as time passes. Bobbitt (1925) continued by noting that factors such as a lack of extra time available to teachers for curriculum planning, the over-specialization of teachers in their subject areas, and the uncertainty of the school's function for the community also prevent curricular reformation (pp. 664-665). Moreover, the irrelevance of the curriculum to the students' home lives causes further difficulty in the pursuit of curriculum development.

> Even when there is "home work," this home work is merely a device for extending the school work by using an hour or two of the pupil's time at home. It is "school work" in the sense that it is preparation for academic exercises and has

> no relation to the pupil's normal home activities... where schools are thoroughly traditional and isolated from community living, this doctrine is meaningless, and a curriculum committee is relatively helpless, except, of course, to do the traditional thing. (pp. 657-658)

Consequently, the perpetuated activities of the classroom prevent re-thinking of the curriculum, as habit serves to reinforce all aspects of instruction – even that which may be viewed as detrimental to an objective observer from outside the school.

On a more positive note, in pursuing a curriculum that is relevant to the "real life" of the student, the small rural community may have an advantage over larger systems. The homogeneous nature of most rural communities allows for the curriculum to represent the beliefs and values of the area more directly (see Fuller, 1982; Massey and Crosby, 1983; Peshkin, 1992). McIntire, et al. (1990) specifically believed that "the nature of rural communities creates a set of conditions that influence the economic support, physical facilities and staffing and, consequently, the academic experiences of the rural student" (pp. 168-169).

Teachers are a component often left out of the curriculum-making process in rural school systems, as the community will often only hire teachers who will conform to local expectations (Peshkin, 1992, 1978). Church (1988), however, described an instance in which teachers in a rural setting were given nearly complete control of the direction that the local curriculum would take – with seemingly positive results for the school. Called in as a curricular consultant for a school system in rural Nova Scotia, Church suggested that the teachers design a curriculum around the real-life experiences of the children in the area; for, as one teacher noted about the curriculum as it stood, "I can hardly expect these children who have never been in a two-story building to understand about elevators. So much of what we are doing is too far removed from their experiences" (p. 449). Consequently, Church asked the teachers to envision unique aspects of the community at large, and then develop school-wide themes as to how these aspects could be incorporated into a new, relative curriculum for the students. Students began bringing artifacts of personal interest from home and other places. From this, the teachers at the school developed a curriculum that was truly representative of the locale and did meet with the approval of nearly the entire community.

When asking herself what she had learned from the experience, Church stated, "I discovered the power released when teachers are freed to take ownership in the curriculum" (p. 450). That being the case, at least one of two questions must be answered: Where was the input of local residents in the formation of this curriculum that appears to be so prevalent in other rural communities? And, if this situation resulted in a positive curriculum that met the approval of the community, why are not other rural areas empowering their teachers with a "free reign" for designing the curriculum, if such a successful result can be seen here?

Also central to the formation of curriculum is the selection of textbooks by a school system. Furthermore, the actual textbooks and the types of individuals who select them can vary from community to community. Small (1977) found that there was a variance at the state level in this regard as well. Certain systems leave the responsibility of book selection to local school systems entirely; some provide lists of texts that are suggested for use; while still others have lists from which school systems in their state *must* choose. Unfortunately, when textbook selection is done at the local level, one of three undesirable outcomes seems to consistently occur as a result of including small-town parents on textbook selection committees, according to Small:

> - Only a small, hand-picked group of parents are chosen by school officials to assist in text selection (normally, only individuals of advanced education), thus nullifying representation of the entire community;

> - The opposite of the situation above, whereby a deluge of parental input is displayed, and thus the quantity and quality of the input is unmanageable and ineffectual; or

> - The appointment of what Small describes as "a 'dedicated' or 'fanatic' [person]," who is passionate about school policy and is believed to represent a majority of community sentiment on educational philosophy. (p. 125)

The solution that Small offers to the crisis of textbook selection is similar to that offered by Church (1988): allowing teachers to design the curriculum in accord with *principles* set forth by the community, and to let the texts chosen directly reflect those principles. Left unresolved by Small (1977), however, is who should make the decision in the text selection process, as the author does not state (either implicitly or explicitly) whether this responsibility rests with the teacher or the administrators.

Sher (1983) also discussed the idea of empowering the proper stakeholders in curriculum formation. He noted that the decision-making power in the school reform process often rests in a very exclusive group – namely, "a collection of politicians, lawyers, government officials, and highly-placed school administrators within education" (p. 282). However, it is one or more groups of people with the greatest personal stakes in the outcome of the policy, and those with the greatest knowledge of what works for the community and what does not, who are often excluded from the formative dialogue: parents, teachers, principals, and students.

Certain "external forces" may also be at work in the shaping of a school's curriculum, even in the seemingly insulated setting of the rural small town. Kirst and Walker (1971) pointed out that, historically, the curricula of all schools can be superseded by national concerns, and the isolated rural school system is certainly no exception (see also Asplaugh, 1992; Kliebard, 1995a). At the outset of the twentieth century, rural *and* urban schools adjusted their curricula for the "Americanization" of the multitudes of immigrants entering the country. Later, when fascism posed threats to democracy, education for democratic citizenship took center stage in the curriculum of most schools. American involvement in the First and Second World Wars caused a curricular shift towards manual training for war-time purposes. When *Sputnik* was launched, the "national" curriculum changed once again, this time to an emphasis on science, mathematics, and foreign languages as the U.S. attempted to regain its scientific and technological edge. These incidents in history (among many others) have caused widespread re-thinking of the American curriculum, and the pressure for federal unity in a given direction greatly impacted small rural schools – schools that were often far removed from the esoteric issues of national and international intrigue.

Rural Communities and Alternative Curricula

The concept of the hometown student becoming an "entrepreneur" is quite appealing to many rural areas, as such communities often experience a mass exodus of their most high-achieving students for the apparent opportunity of larger cities. Often, the talented student in the small rural town finds little hope for his or her financial future within the locale and will seek new challenges elsewhere. The economic conditions of a rural area also directly affect all aspects of its schools, especially at its most basic core – the curriculum. The impoverished state of many rural schools has prompted them to reduce their teaching staffs, thus trimming elective components of the curriculum available to their students. In a study conducted by Gardener (1984), for example, the prevailing obstacle for school success among 162 rural districts in Montana was school financing for electives in the curriculum. To partially alleviate funding difficulties associated with curriculum development, one particular strategy has been shown over the past two decades to help. Schools with distance education capabilities (through either television, computer, or both) can offer courses which normally do not warrant the hiring of a full- or even part-time teacher in the subject (Barker & Hall, 1998; Barker, 1990; Joiner et al., 1981; Lundgren, 1985; Siegmund & McFadden, 1985; Worthy, 1988). However, such capabilities themselves cost a great deal of money, even if expenses are shared among several communities. Thus, the necessity of assistance from institutions of higher education may come into play. Schmidt, et al. (1994) claimed that cooperation between universities and local school districts can enhance curricular opportunities for rural students. A program sponsored by the University of Texas at Austin uses distance technologies to teach algebra to migrant children. The author cites that the needs associated with expanding the rural curriculum through distance learning technologies must be met in a three-fold manner: 1) The content of the course must *motivate* the students to attend the sessions; 2) the course must be *sequenced* in a way that addresses the wide variance in abilities associated with rural students; and 3) social skills must be prioritized through maximizing the interaction the students experience in the course (pp. 61-62). Within this framework (and with funding and training for local school staff), distance education can certainly enhance the curricular offerings of an isolated school system, or simply offer basic courses to those with no previous formal education.

Many schools have utilized astounding creativity and determination to acquire things that many would consider "extracurricular." In some cases, rural schools have undergone comprehensive changes in their academic organization in an effort to augment the curriculum available to their students (see Hadley and Wood, 1987; Hutto, 1990; Joiner et al., 1981; Yoder, 1985). Beaumont (1995) discusses his experiences in this regard as a high school English teacher in rural southwest Mississippi. He came to the school wishing to start a student newspaper and envisioned improving the entire school simultaneously. With a budget that was already stretched to the limit and local businesses already having supported the schools as much as they could, Beaumont turned a dream into a reality. Along the way, he enlisted community involvement, inter-departmental cooperation within the school, and enthusiastic industry on the part of the students. The newspaper club raised its own funds, used ordinary essays in English class for feature articles, solicited the math classes to help figure manageable budgets for the club, and hired students from business and marketing classes to circulate the newspaper around town. This interactive attitude seemed to perpetuate itself. Beaumont noted that the "climate" of the school improved drastically as a result of newspaper projects (since its introduction in 1992), that community support for the school has increased, and the newspaper has produced more multi-grade interaction among students in the building (p. 27). The ingenuity of Beaumont and his students, immersed in an otherwise-deprived setting, set off a chain reaction of positive effects for the school and town in this rural area.

In a separate area of rural Mississippi, yet another innovative curriculum has brought hope to a place was also experiencing economic crisis. The river delta region in the west-central part of the state has given rise to the Quality Education Project (QEP), a plan instituted by former Governor Ray Marbus and State Superintendent of Education Richard Boyd which finally came to fruition in the early 1990s (Lovelady, 1992). Within the plan, seven districts in this region received funding from the U.S. Department of Education to empower their communities through involvement with the local schools. The plan emphasizes the following objectives:

- To garner and maintain community support of schools;

- To provide research-based training for parents and school staff in home-school communications and parenting skills; and

- Provide material support for future programs that the QEP wishes to implement. (p. 56)

Reading was promoted as the curricular focus in the schools involved with the QEP, through which an enhanced dialogue between the home and school is sought. Despite still lacking many of the resources necessary for a competitive educational system, the people in the areas served by the QEP have, at the very least, developed a bond between themselves and their schools, and fostered a healthy dialogue between their children's learning and their home lives. This is another example of the creativity of citizens in a rural area and how they helped ease the financial shortfalls that are a daily reality.

Nachtigal (1982) cited yet another example of community outreach action at work in rural Mississippi with the establishment of the Holmes County Teacher Corps Project, in an area where most of the teachers are produced by Mississippi Valley State University in Itta Bena. The Holmes County School Superintendent, William Dean, approached MVSU with needs for "higher student achievement, curriculum change in the schools, and the addressing of community problems and concerns" (p. 52). Out of these needs emerged the Teacher Corps, which worked to increase the dialogue transpiring between the home and school on matters of curriculum, instruction, evaluation, and interactive school-community projects. The Corps was comprised of teachers who visited students' homes, developed personal relationships with parents, and invited their input on curricular and instructional strategies. Despite the profound poverty of the area, the residents felt a rejuvenated connection to their children's schools; the ownership of the local curriculum became theirs, and the priorities that the community valued became its most vital components – an interdependence that continues to this day.

Sometimes overlooked in the developmental process of the rural curriculum are the need for vocational education and other elective areas that may interest students. The isolated nature of many rural school systems may cause them to be "bypassed" when such services are allocated. However, in western South Dakota, a program known as the Black Hills Special Services Cooperative (BHSSC) has been successful in providing effective vocational training for interested students. The BHSSC staff and students look to improve local businesses and organizations by producing new goods that will benefit the area. According to Baumeister and Morris (1992), three components made the BHSSC program successful in delivering effective vocational training to rural students in the region: flexible and dynamic programs that can be adapted to meet the individual and unique needs of students, school districts, communities, and private businesses; cooperation and coordination with school districts, public agencies, private businesses, and the community to foster the development of needed services; and creativity and innovation in finding solutions to identified problems (p. 43). Often left to die with equipment and training that are generations old, vocational education in outlying rural areas is receiving a boost from programs such as the BHSSC – bringing not only improved training to the students, but improved interaction between the community and school as well.

Contemporary Rural Teacher Perspectives on Curriculum Development

Many modern American school systems have considered the advantages of site-based management, or the decentralization of larger school units into organizations run at the building level (Bachus, 1992; Brown, et al., 1996; Kannapel, et al., 1995; Powell, 1991). The intimacy of a local environment (it is assumed) would foster a more beneficial academic product for the students in a given area. Critical to such a strategy, therefore, is the active participation of all stakeholders – namely teachers, administrators, students, parents, and the community – in all facets of a school's operation. It is reasonable to assume that, even in the most promising of such environments, certain individuals will not wish to take as active a role as others. Consequently, the enthusiasm of their participation will be unique to only certain aspects of the school's operation (for example, a father's special interest in athletics may lend his involvement to this portion of the school's program, while his interest may wane in other areas). Herzog and Pittman (1995) asserted that "a key to success in education reform is the school staff, and yet university education programs have done little to provide educators with specialized training for work in rural areas" (p. 114). So while the superintendent or principal may organize a carefully-conceived system of involvement for all stakeholders, this variable is bound to surface.

Similarly, teachers who are *coerced* into participating in curriculum development or revision may not provide full effort in such a project. While reflection upon the curriculum may be an unwritten responsibility when accepting a teaching job, many teachers would rather have the curriculum provided for them and are indifferent about having any input as to its contents. This was shown in the study by Bachus (1992), as he sampled 67 teachers in rural school districts with fewer than 600 students in the K-12 grades. Only 48% of the respondents wished to take part in the "instructional organization and implementation of the curriculum" (p. 2). All of the schools from which Bachus drew his samples were new participants in site-based management plans, heaping more responsibility on each staff member than had previously been the case.

Likewise, McCracken and Miller (1988) examined 24 teachers in four rural secondary schools about their perceived roles in curriculum development. All teachers understood that, in working in rural environments, the number of responsibilities they would have were greater. However, when asked about their willingness to participate in curriculum development, a majority of the teachers disliked this duty, even though they were aware of its importance. Kannapel, et al. (1995) conducted a similar study in Kentucky. Four rural school districts undergoing a new site-based management program in this state were studied. It was found that the local committees in charge of these programs had difficulty in achieving what they considered "true shared decision making" (p. 23). According to Uhl, et al. (1993), who surveyed 290 rural school superintendents, principals, and school board members in South Dakota, most administrators and board members preferred *not* to implement shared decision making on curriculum and other issues due to limitations in human resources.

Despite this general negative feeling by rural teachers towards curriculum work, evidence also exists of improvements being made to assist these individuals in this task. Benson (1996) discussed the Bread Loaf Rural Teacher Network, a national organization of rural teachers interested in school reform. The group focused on challenges that rural teachers face in creating curriculum and suggested community-wide discussions in rural areas for producing curricula that is representative of the particular locales.

Powell (1991) also offers suggestions for enhancing shared decision making for teachers in rural schools, particularly in regard to curriculum. He prompts administrators to focus on three ideas: 1) The establishment of a "goal-setting session" before the start of the school year, either at a regular faculty meeting or a casual restaurant gathering; 2) for particularly small staffs, the establishment of a 3-5 member teacher council on curricular matters, diverse in subject areas, who would report directly to the principal on issues and faculty concerns; and 3) as much delegation of duties to teachers as possible (p. 12). As noted in the last suggestion, Powell recognizes the need for teachers in small schools to maintain multiple responsibilities. The type of teacher needed for such an operation, he contends, is one who is "self-directed":

> A staff member who is self-directed and effective might view his or her principal as open and participative, while another less autonomous staff member may accuse the same principal of being uncooperative and unreceptive. (pp. 11-12)

However, it must be remembered that teachers do not always wish to have these responsibilities, despite the fact these may be understood components of their jobs when signing their contracts.

Evidence suggests that both new and experienced teachers are often wary of being alone in the curriculum development process. In a study of (at the time) one the few remaining one-room, one-teacher rural schoolhouses, Glen (1980) noted that the lone teacher was hesitant about making choices for the curriculum. A county system of organization oversaw the school but did not provide input for the curriculum. Dealing with a relatively uneducated clientele, the teacher also could not turn to the townspeople for assistance with curricular choices. The teacher mentioned that, despite her twenty-two years of experience in education, she felt unqualified to make curricular decisions that were up-to-date with contemporary times. That this was a daunting task is understandable; and it is the predicament of many contemporary rural schools, where one staff member comprises the entire department for most academic areas.

Summary

With limited funds and human resources, many rural schools have had to exercise great creativity in providing a well-rounded curriculum for their students. In many cases, this has involved teachers in rural schools having to assume multiple roles. For as a small-town doctor or lawyer must usually become a "generalist" in many facets of medicine or law, so must a small-town teacher be prepared to assume a wide variety of jobs – some of which may be first-time challenges. In addition to the extra duties that such teachers face, educators in the rural sector are also faced with all of the traditional roles, not the least of which being conventional curriculum-making. Administrators in rural areas, as in other parts of the country, have experienced resistance to these efforts. Is this resistance to curricular reform in rural areas due to an inert populace unwilling to shift from perennial customs? Or is it the result of teaching staff that, for the most part, might be viewed as non-progressive? Or is it a combination of these factors, or others?

It has been said that sheer knowledge available to the world is doubling every 15 years at the current pace; it is also theorized that half of what human beings will need to know *simply to survive* in the year 2200 is not yet known today. Whatever the statistics may say, it is reasonable to conclude that the world is transforming itself at a rapid pace never seen before. The decisions that curriculum-makers deduce, therefore, are more important than ever. And these decisions are even more crucial in rural schools, as the supposed "change agents" – that is, the teachers who propose curricular revision and development – face a local agenda that is not often so swift to change. Many factors enter into play to cause this resistance in rural areas, and some of these will now be discussed.

7. Athletics, Consolidation, and the Hidden Curriculum of the American Small Town

Nothing bleeds quite like devotion.

– Unknown

Warmth may be a word to describe small-town affinity to its school athletic teams. When the high school football team is at home on a crisp Friday night in autumn, there is warmth to be found in snuggling close to a neighbor in the stands, with a cozy blanket being shared. Come the winter months, warmth is found in the gymnasium; everyone's pick-up truck winds its way through the snowy roads to arrive at the school, a comfortable venue so well-heated that the ten performers on the floor run around in shorts, and everyone watching is impervious to the sub-zero temperatures outside.

The "warmth" that these spectators feel may also be spiritual, however, as the team symbolizes a local pride and identity associated with the school and community. To be sure, few things tie a rural town to its character like athletics. It transcends the generations of families in the town; the grandsons of superstars are now the stars themselves, and those who can remember long ago compare the descendant to the ancestor. The continuity of the game, be it football, basketball, or baseball, crosses over the decades and bears witness to the surrounding change of the community. Whether the football field has seen a shopping mall or new housing rise and fall around it, or has seen the withering of unkempt buildings around it, the field is still one hundred yards long like it was one hundred years ago.

Thus, athletics positions itself as perhaps the most influential element in the formation of the hidden curriculum for a community. Since local pride is often predicated on little else, the individual and collective success of sports in a given small town is the barometer of choice. Great value is placed – for better or worse – on the athletic performances that the young people of the town "bring to the table." Expectations begin at an early age, and thus carry with it the aspect of the unspoken expectations in the community. The expectations are not formally taught in the early grades, nor they are not posted on the bulletin board at the public library. Rather, they are carried in the virtual oxygen of the community. In casual discussions at restaurants, churches, and grocery stores, the topic is raised; the topic is also raised in the way former, current, and future athletes carry themselves around town.

As Apple (1975) described, the hidden curriculum sets transparent "boundaries" for the young people of a community, letting them know what the parameters are for acceptable behavior. "The hidden curriculum in schools serves to reinforce basic rules surrounding the nature of conflict and its uses. It posits a network of assumptions that, when internalized by students, establishes the boundaries of legitimacy" (p. 99). This sentiment is echoed by Peshkin (1978), who in his description of "Mansfield" portrays the importance of a football evening in a small Ohio town.

> Approach Mansfield from any direction on any one of five Friday nights in fall and you will see, even while still a considerable distance away, a bright glow illuminating the dark sky... they [the lights] stand like giants at attention guarding the school district's football field and the very small town adjacent to it. People say Mansfield is a football town, and they are right. No other activity elicits the same degree of devotion and support... more than 40 percent of all local persons standing and sitting under the Friday night lights, being seen, running with friends around

the refreshment stand, strolling on the track that encircles
the field, and even watching the game. (p. 45)

To be sure, the big football or basketball game – regardless
if one is a fan or not – is the one event in town that everyone knows
about. Often, the stores downtown will be closed on gameday or
gamenight, or they will be empty anyway. The games serve as the
most complete "town meetings" that the community has to offer. If
there is someone you need to talk to, you will find him or her at the
game. It may take you until mid-way through the third quarter, but
you *will* eventually see the person. Perhaps a handful of "true" fans
are intently watching every play, but the rest are visiting with each
other, catching up, gossiping, while still physically "being there" as a
representative of the community for the home team. Perhaps the
players' parents are the only ones who know which kids are playing
regularly and which ones aren't, and they let the coach know these
observations in a holler from a few rows deep in the stands.

The stakeholders of the local team, however, go far beyond
the players, parents, and coaches. Everyone from the coal miner to
the baker to the barber (who might give free haircuts to team
members after a win, as seen in the movie *Hoosiers*) owns a share of
"stock" in the club. For it is at local athletic contests that the
American rural town truly comes together. It is the best chance to
"catch up" local news.

Basketball, The Hidden Curriculum, and Small-Town Indiana

If one extracurricular-interscholastic activity envelops one
region, it is high school basketball in Indiana. When one hears the
very word – "Indiana" – its commanding tone conjures images of a
state-full of history and talent for the game. Former Indiana
University head basketball coach Bob Knight, who was at the school
for nearly thirty years and won three national championships, perhaps
summed it up best when he said, "There is no greater place for the
game. Basketball may have been invented in Massachusetts, but it
was made for Indiana."

It would certainly seem so, as one takes the beautiful scenic
path down State Road 46. The route, which passes through Knight's
hallowed Assembly Hall at IU in Bloomington, stretches east to west
across the state. In its entirety, one wanders through or past the little
towns of Spencer, Elletsville, Nashville, Bloomfield, Linton, Milan,

and many others. Some do not even seem to be actual towns, but mere curves in the road. Nonetheless, at these curves one usually sees an old family barn with a crude basketball hoop attached to the front of the wall. If Norman Rockwell needed to encapsulate Indiana in one portrait, it may well have been the image of the young farm boy tossing the ball towards this hoop in his overalls. The little man continues to fire away, literally hitting the side of the barn more often than the rim itself. Night falls as he continues to try, and his parents call out to him to come inside. "One more shot – please?" he responds through the dark.

Perhaps nowhere is this culture more prevalent than on the *backroads* of Indiana, where for a century basketball has remained the measuring stick for local identity. As Martin (1998) notes, there is a "close, emotional relationship between the community and high school basketball in rural and small-town Indiana... the association of basketball with Indiana is central to the culture of schools and communities and is a source of identification and pride for the state and the region" (p. 121). Unlike its neighbors to the east (namely, Ohio and Pennsylvania), where larger communities allowed for the more complex and expensive sport of football to develop, little places such as Dugger, Indiana still need only five young men to represent the town for the coming winter. In some seasons, the five young men might consist of only freshmen and sophomores, and the team "takes it lumps" from more experienced outfits; in future years, however, the local five develops strength and cohesiveness, and becomes the powerhouse that their youthful potential had promised just a couple of seasons prior.

As *Hoosiers* actress Barbara Hershey said of her beloved hometown of "Neosho" in Indiana, "Neosho" also does not appear on many Indiana state maps (as in the movie, a pseudonym is being used for this community as well). For sure, you can go to a public library in the state, pull out an imposing atlas, and find the coordinates. But for the most part, Neosho is basically known as another one of those "curves in the road" between Bloomington and Indianapolis. As will be seen later in this book, most business and industry has departed, and Neosho High School has been threatened by the state with consolidation on numerous occasions. Time and time again, Neosho has had to prove to the Indiana State Board of Education that it can survive on its own, not just "curricularly" but financially, with an ever-decreasing tax revenue structure. Yet, each time they do indeed manage to stave it off, and one more year of "educating our own kids" can be enjoyed. More importantly to most, though, is that another season of Neosho basketball can be enjoyed as well – so long as five qualified boys can be found to take the floor come early December.

If any historical evidence is needed to prove the importance of basketball to Neosho, one needs to look no further than the gymnasium itself. It was built in 1927, exactly twenty years after the adjoining high school was constructed. And, the gymnasium remains the lone structural improvement to the grounds in the past 60 years. The population of Neosho, due to a number of factors, has remained mostly stable throughout the decades; small economic booms and busts have kept the figure right around 400, give or take a few at any time. There is no football team, so unlike Peshkin's Mansfield, no blinding lights of any sort greet entrants into the town. It is sleepy, quiet, and nearly lifeless, with the exception of one building on selected Friday and Saturday nights in the winter.

The concept of Indiana high school basketball, in being reduced to single word, is *pride*. Pride, as defined by Webster, is characterized as "reasonable or justifiable self-respect." Beyond individual self-respect, however, it is a concept that connects people – not only with a geographical place, but with a heritage as well. It suggests that there is something present that is worth preserving, defending, and advancing. Pride in something is pride in one's self and one's surroundings; in other words, to be proud of something is to claim to be part of it – past, present, or future. When one speaks of "community pride," it refers to not only the characteristics *shared* by the community members, but also the unique additions that each individual member contributes to it. Because of this phenomenon, a community thus remains static and yet metamorphic at the same time. Similarly, the pride that the community holds shifts as well, but also remains constant with the things that have stood the test of time in the community. Things that are typically constant easily come to mind: church, family living, local workplaces, and athletics, to name a few. All of these can be sources of pride to varying degrees in all communities, large or small.

In colloquial terms, basketball in Indiana and football in Ohio are often referred to as "religions." Assuredly, citizens in those states (as examples) follow these sports "religiously" in the adverbial use of the word. Moreover, it may be argued that these entities *are* in essence "religions," with the word being used as a noun. They have leaders or pastors (coaches) to tend to the congregation (fans) by sending a certain message. This is done through the use of the church building and ornaments (stadiums, goal posts, etc), to follow a certain life path. But more so, as is the case in sectarian religions, secular "religions" go a great distance in defining the very essence of an individual or a community. A religion, in any sense of the word, speaks of customs, values, traditions, songs, sacred artifacts, and honored figures of those individuals and communities, as well as black marks of transgressions against that religion. Those who desecrate or blaspheme against the religion are outcasts, whereas those who follow it faithfully are rewarded with a permanent place in its future (e.g. lifelong fan / "everlasting life"). And, as in sectarian religion, it requires a day-to-day faithfulness – and in some cases, it permeates every moment of the day for an individual.

This comparison is brought for example purposes only; for most football-crazed Ohio State University fans or followers of the basketball Hoosiers in Bloomington, Indiana can separate the religion from the Religion, the mundane from the mystical, the natural from the Supernatural. Yet, in terms of defining a town, a county, a region, or an entire state, the impact is evident. It is indeed part of the "hidden curriculum"; for an English teacher in small-town Indiana will have tough time fitting in, regardless of skill in teaching Shakespeare, if he or she doesn't like basketball.

In the same sense, conventional religion also serves to define most rural areas and towns, and thus also contributes heavily to the hidden curriculum of what is taught in the local public school. For centuries, rural areas have been honored for "country values"; that is to say, the Puritan Work Ethic and honest labor that always seems to come from such places. While this is certainly true, the underlying moral structure between any two rural communities – even two that are geographically close together – may be extraordinarily different. It is one of the factors involved in the fight of many rural citizens against modern school consolidation, which will now be discussed. There is often a wariness of people from one town of those from a neighboring community, and the influence these "strangers" may have over the children if they are sent to school there.

Taken for a Ride: The Unseen Costs of Modern Rural School Consolidation and the Curriculum

An important town meeting is taking place at the high school that mother and father need to attend. The state has come to the town, seeking to consolidate the local high school with a neighboring one. What is promised, the state agents claim, are expanded resources and opportunities for the local students; as the current high school sits, they claim, it cannot function with the dwindling tax base of the community, and is too old to repair at a reasonable cost.

The townspeople began wandering into the high school. Like a game night, their numbers are great; unlike a game night, their spirits are low and their speculation is fearful. They filter into the school's auditorium as some city-slickers in business suits scuffle some charts up on the stage and share laughs with each other. The local school superintendent is also on the stage, mingling with the strangers. Next in marches the school board, not so formally dressed. The local board consists of five older men. One of the few students attending the meeting turns to his father and asks, "Pa, who are those people that just came in?" His father responds, "Those are the school board men. They make decisions about what goes on in your school." Actually further confused, boy asks his father, "Well Pa, how did they get that job? I bet they get to make a lot of important decisions." In a storm of mixed emotions, the father answered, "Most of 'em were put there long ago by one of their brothers or uncles or something. They just get to be there by knowing somebody." The boy turns his head the other direction, satisfied with the answer his father gave him. The father then mumbles something to himself.

Over the next hour, the people from the state use some words like "fiscal management," "curricular expansion," and "performance-based assessment," but it didn't sound anything familiar about the school that townspeople had previously known or currently knew. When the final speaker from the state finished his speech, he gave a small smile and a quick nod to affirm the accuracy of his previous statements and those of his colleagues. Moreover, his smile and nod seemed to tell the town that they were no longer making correct decisions about their schools, and the correct view had just been given.

Rural community sentiment against consolidation has been in existence since the Committee of Twelve suggested its widespread implementation in 1897. Some of this sentiment has been unfairly attributed to a general static nature of the rural resident. An example of this is shared by Cubberly (1912).

> "The chief reason for this [feeling] is that the improvement must be initiated and carried through by the votes of the rural residents themselves. This makes it very difficult of accomplishment, because, as a class, farmers and residents of little villages are extremely conservative, unprogressive, jealous, penny-wise, and lacking in any proper conception of the value of good educational conditions... new ideas come to them but slowly; what has been for a long time is good enough. No better evidence of this is needed than the stubbornness with which the consolidation movement has been resisted by country people. (p. 12)

Cubberly's statement is obviously sweeping, and perhaps only partially accurate. However, when the cultures of different value systems clash, it can indeed produced mired educational results, as noted by he continues. "The lack of coordination and cooperation between the districts is one of the most serious obstacles to the consolidation movement... the people [school boards] represent are often swayed more by envy and jealousy – personal, political, religious, social, economic – than by all of the educational arguments that can be advanced" (p. 40).

These localized battles over consolidation have continued into modern times. A focus group has been established in West Virginia by concerned parents of rural school children, known as "Challenge West Virginia." According to Eckman (2000), the consolidation of schools in West Virginia continued at a fast pace through the end of the century, and has often closed community schools in favor of new, isolated campuses that are out of the way for everyone. "Students reported that their schedules only allowed them to see working parents on the weekends. Others noted that they avoid higher-level classes because after a 10 or 11-hour school day, they simply don't have more time in the evenings for the extra homework. One student testified that she spends 32 percent of her school day riding a bus. Even young students may have to spend stretches of unsupervised time waiting for bus transfers" (p. 2). Despite evidence to the contrary, conventional wisdom continues to seemingly convince the public that "bigger is better." In Texas, for example, research has shown that anywhere from one-fourth to one-half of students are in schools whose achievement would likely improve if the schools were smaller, and would conversely grow worse if the schools were larger. (ibid.)

The initial furious wave of consolidation that swept through American education in the first half of the twentieth century left an indelible mark. As Theobald (1993) stated, "After 1918, the number of country schools and students began to decline. This trend never stopped, and, as a result, there are fewer than one thousand one-room schools in existence today" (p. 132). The 117,108 school *districts* that existed in the United States in 1940 had decreased 87% to 15,367 in 1993, due mostly to continued consolidation efforts in the latter portion of the century (Theobald, 1993). As noted earlier, however, this policy was not smoothly implemented in all rural areas; many communities wished to maintain the intimate structure of their small, hometown schools.

Small schools have often been commended by those who claim their structure and operation are beneficial to the learning process (Gregory & Smith, 1987; Odden & Wohlstetter, 1995). Whether the school is small in an "indigenous" sense (the product of simply being in a small town) or is small in a "manufactured" sense (the product of decentralization, as has happened in many large city school districts), such an environment is seen to potentially provide an arena of intimacy, caring, and quality personal interaction. Many small rural schools have withstood currents and counter-currents of school reform, such as consolidation and decentralization, over the course of educational history. Consequently, an interesting dichotomy results. The smallness of a rural school (in terms of enrollment and space) would seemingly present a workable venue for reform, especially in regard to curriculum. However, small rural communities often are also among the most resistant to most kinds of change, and are not swayed by the many educational "fads" often presented by policymakers – particularly those that come from outside of their locale or from teachers new to the district (Clarke & Hood, 1986; Nachtigal, 1982; Porter, 1996; Seal & Harmon, 1995; Shaw, 1991). And as in Fleming's (1995) example of the consolidation fight in Ohio, Weiler (1994) speaks of similar "outside power structures" in the formative periods of the western United States. "Rural school reform in California in the period 1900-1940 was motivated by many of the same concerns that underlay the national movement to reform rural education... the expansion of state regulations and control over the work of teachers" (p. 25).

Stripping small, rural communities of their once-unchallenged autonomy has often met with fierce resistance, as "outsiders" prescribe what they presume to be a better education for the children of the locale. As Fleming (1995) discussed, many small towns in the Midwest built the cultures of their communities around the traditional one-room schoolhouse; parents held a much more interactive role with their children's teachers and the school building itself served as much more than simply a pedagogical forum – town meetings, social gatherings, and other necessary village functions were held in the schoolhouse. The building stood as a reflection of the community that called the school its own, and was the axis upon which the vitality of the area revolved. Furthermore, the curriculum was the principle upon which the building stood; as Friedberger (1996) asserts, "In rural America a curriculum was designed that connected country schools to the concerns of rural life" (p. 151). Even today in many small towns, the community calendar is often constructed around the school calendar, including events such as banquets, holiday pageants, and athletic contests, among others.

The question of "autonomy versus consolidation" continues today. Odden and Wohlstetter (1995) supported the idea of site-based management with the argument that "a broader range of perspectives" for the local school will meet the individual needs of a given community in a more appropriate fashion (p. 33). With the idea of consolidation, professionals in the education field have offered an expanded curriculum and range of opportunities for the citizens of the small town. In the traditional sense of consolidation, it was believed that a virtual pooling of resources would allow the rural school curriculum to expand for every student in a given region and leave no child out of a comprehensive education. Over time, as Fleming (1995) pointed out, those involved in the issue of consolidation became extremely mistrustful of each other; the educators felt that local townspeople did not have the knowledge (or access to the knowledge) to properly run the schools, and the citizens of the town feared the corruption of their children's values by those of the neighboring community into which they would be integrated. Dunne (1982) observed a similar occurrence in Iowa, where the resistance to consolidation appeared as strong as in Ohio:

Iowa Falls, for example, has suffered from declining enrollments, too; they could easily absorb the 470 children in the Alden school district.

Unfortunately, this does not appeal to the citizens and parents of Alden's school children, nor to the residents of more than 200 other Iowa school districts. Alden wants its children in Alden, not in Iowa Falls "where nobody knows them." (p. 257)

Despite local disapproval in most places, however, consolidation proved to be one of the most widely-implemented educational policies in twentieth-century America. Haller and Monk (1988) contended that this assimilation into larger and larger units may have provided new-found financial and curricular enhancement for some small rural school systems, but the enlargement of the school that these children attended may have actually imposed a disservice on their *social* development. This disservice, they state, continues in the consolidated schools of today:

On the one hand, there is an unmistakable congruence between the long-standing effort to consolidate small rural schools and the "hard" dimension of the current school improvement effort, with its emphasis on enhanced academic offerings and accountability. Officials in state education offices across the land can be expected to resonate these calls for improved, cost-efficient programs. It is an old and re-assuring refrain to the ears of those in positions of power.

On the other hand, there is *no* comparable congruence between the consolidation movement and the "soft" side of the modern reform effort, with its emphasis on the social development of youth, keeping schools close to their communities, increased parent involvement, and decentralized decision-making. These are new to the landscape of state education officials, and there is no tradition into which they can comfortably fit. Indeed, these ideas are, in many respects, antithetical to some of their more cherished beliefs. (p. 479)

Thus, in terms of modeling a citizen for a democratic society, the side effects of consolidation may actually contribute to social regression in the lives of rural school children. While their *tangible* resources for social mobility are being bolstered (money, resources, increased course offerings, etc.), their opportunities for experiences with social interaction are being lessened; the close, personal nature of a small school system is lost within the larger framework. With much of the rest of the educational world pursuing community activism and pride, political autonomy for decision making, and more *personal* interaction among children at schools, this human side of school reform is not facilitated with the consolidation model. It may, in fact, be antithetical to these so-called "inherent values" of what the curriculum of a school in a democracy should entail.

Retention of Quality Rural School Teachers, School Buildings, and School Programs

As discussed earlier, the teacher had near complete control of the curriculum in the American classroom – urban, rural, or otherwise – before 1900. This forced a wide dispersion of content, with a lack of alignment in what being taught from place to place. To further exacerbate this problem in country areas, quality individuals did not always find their ways to rural classrooms. Thus, before the recommendations of the Committee of Ten, children in an isolated rural setting were often at the mercy of a teacher ignorant in national (or even local) curricular trends. Since the beginnings of public education in the United States, rural schools have not been the brightest beacon for attracting teachers pursuing their professional careers. Even part of what Ellwood Cubberly was discussing in 1912 rings painfully true today.

> Before the growth of the cities, the rural school had almost as good a chance to employ the best available teachers as the village or small town school. The opportunity has greatly decreased under modern circumstances. The country school cannot attract the best-trained teachers. It recruits from the least effectively trained, and it rapidly loses the more capable and brilliant teachers, who are first promoted to the village schools, then to town schools, and finally to the great city system where pay, tenure, pensions, and the graded school attract them. Thus the rural school

teachers of today are as a whole the least experienced and
the least competent of the teaching body. (pp.vi-vii)

The unattractiveness of rural schools for some more
qualified teachers is obviously a double-edged sword. The schools
themselves experience an attrition rate that turns over up to half of
their teaching staffs each year; students are annually unsure if their
teachers will be there the following term. In addition to the negative
effect on students, this problem causes logistical difficulties for the
rest of the staff. A large contingent of new employees needing to be
trained each year puts a strain on the time allocations of duties for the
veterans, and it becomes nearly impossible to build a sense of
cohesiveness within the staff.

Typically, rural schools become the safety valve for new
teachers who cannot find jobs at more "desirable" schools. Higher-
paying positions that have been traditionally reserved at urban and
suburban districts are filled quickly, and often by experienced
teachers who simply switch from one district to another. These
lucrative jobs become the objectives of the new teacher in the rural
school, and after one, two, or three years, they leave the rural school
in pursuit of more money (and presumed) better locations. After the
2000-2001 school year in Illinois alone, 28% of the first-year teachers
in consolidated and unconsolidated rural K-12 schools had left their
jobs before beginning their second years (Illinois State Board of
Education, 2001).

According to Feldmann (2000), new teachers have a variety
of reasons for wanting or not wanting to pursue positions in rural
schools. For many, there is a perception of safety in rural
communities, as well as a more close-knit feeling among the
residents. However, this close-knit feeling may also carry over into a
"fishbowl" effect, whereby the teacher feels that every aspect of his
or her professional *and* personal life is being scrutinized. Therefore,
some may prefer the more anonymous presence of teaching in a
larger community, and thereby compromising a certain degree of
safety and knowledge of neighbors.

Even finding qualified substitute teachers is especially
difficult for contemporary rural schools. For example, while noting
that 15 of the state of Nevada's 17 counties are considered rural,
Matranga, et. al (1995) found that for the 1994-95 school year, none
of the 15 could find a *lone* reliable substitute teacher for its schools.

Often times, principals have to fill in classes for teachers who are absent, or the other teachers need to share the extra load for the day.

The maintenance of quality wider-school programs is obviously central to the development of an effective curriculum. Eisner (1990) has stated that "good curriculum materials both emancipate and educate teachers" (p. 65). In other words, they should be free to develop their own "stories" about curriculum while at the same time learning as their stories develop. Anecdotal use of information can particularly assist the rural school teacher in this regard. The local stories that arise can serve as a curricular component in the rural school. Zellermayer (1997) supports this view when he notes, "The compound act of teaching and telling helps the teacher give shape to new, more complex pedagogical knowledge" (p. 211). In a like manner, Uhrmacher (1997) suggests that there is a "shadow" constantly alongside any curriculum that is used; in other words, he suggests that all curricula gives off a residue of components that is both enabling and disabling to both teachers and students.

From where, then, do programs for good curriculum come from for rural schools? A majority of educators have concluded that it is wise to choose from a variety of areas. Tyler (1949) suggested that "no single source of information is adequate to provide a basis for wise and comprehensive decisions about the objectives of the school" (p. 8). Certainly, this advice is applicable to schools in all areas. Included among these various sources, propose Sadker and Sadker (1988), are parent and community groups, school administrators, federal, state, and local governments, colleges and universities, national tests, educational commissions, and professional organizations, among others.

While much is made of the deterioration of city school buildings, none more decrepit will be found than in rural areas of the country. As formal education was taking root in the early 1900s, and the infamous "field school" precariously stood along the roadsides, little effort was made to ensure that rural school buildings would last any significant amount of time. The typical rural school was described by Cubberly (1912) as "a miserable, unsanitary box" (p. 13). Little progress at all had been seen over the entire nineteenth century, as claimed by Charles Skinner, State Superintendent of Instruction of New York (NEA, 1903):

> Said Whittier [a poet of the age]: '"Still sits the schoolhouse by the road, a ragged beggar sunning." How many school grounds today are fit only for such a "ragged beggar!" Fifty-eight years ago a school officer in New York referred to a large number of schoolhouses in his district as "miserable apologies with gaping roofs, yawning walls, stilted benches, highway playgrounds, and, in fine, every accompaniment calculated to make them all objects most loathsome and repulsive to the juvenile mind." Has the half-century or more of experience and progress wholly removed these conditions? (p. 90)

And, if one looks closely, it will be found that little progress has been made in the past one hundred years as well. Tax funding, naturally, has long been the main hurdle for rural school construction. In a statement that may ring true with many today, Cubberly (1912) further claimed that "good schools are generally impossible under the local taxation system" (p. 19). For some reason that never seems to be discussed, schools in rural areas that do not have significant industry to form a tax base are left to decay. Politicians and so-called community leaders continue to chant that "our children and their education come first," but somehow they continue to let the children be educated in structures in which no president of a company would be caught seen – structures without air conditioning, sometimes without plumbing, and even sometimes without roofs.

Yet, it is still said that "we value education." Why is it, then, that some schools must beg for air conditioning? While Corporate America would not tolerate five minutes without this temperature control, it is somehow seen as an unwarranted "luxury" for our public schools.

Summary

In the definition of the American rural town, interscholastic athletics has long been the platform upon which a place stakes its identity. Be it basketball in the small villages of Illinois or Indiana or football in the larger rural communities of Ohio and Pennsylvania, high school sports provide multiple remedies for the rigors of agrarian life: a chance to catch up on local news, a chance to be seen, and a chance to be seen supporting the town, to name a few. It is truly one of the few remaining private elements of identity for rural citizens, and it is a major reason that school consolidation is deflected so fervently.

The paradigms of federal and state agencies and bureaucracies in conceptualizing the nature of rural communities have often led to poorly-fitting, standardized policy for agrarian schools. Local school control, which is passionately valued by many rural citizens, has been eroded by consolidation and other industrial templates for education. Over the previous one hundred years of consolidation history, a grave mistrust has grown on each side of the issue. In one camp are the education professionals who provided the state-of-the-art recommendations for the residents of the "uncultured" rural areas, people who the professionals felt were unable to make informed, productive educational decisions on their own; and the local residents of rural communities in the other, who sought to maintain the culture of their communities by resisting consolidation, "outsider philosophy," and change in general. It may be argued that, in the past century, this particular tension has been at the core of rural school curricular reform. Rural citizens have been reluctant to embrace strange new instructional strategies for their schools, while educators in these areas have struggled to provide a school experience that would prepare the students for the fast-paced world they will ultimately encounter.

It is reasonable to conclude, therefore, that the local culture of each individual rural community must be acknowledged for school policy to be effectively implemented. Whereas farming may dominate the economy in one small town, for example, milling or mining may dominate in the next; such a simple difference can alter the social structure in two communities which, on the surface, may seem almost identical. If the major religious sect in a small town is constituted of parishioners of a Baptist church, the curriculum that the citizens endorse in their children's education may differ drastically from the next community down the road, where the Roman Catholic church is attended by most residents. The history of American education is marked by misguided efforts at the national and state levels to force-fit policy on a wide scale into the rural communities of the nation – communities which, despite popular opinion, are nearly as diverse as their number.

In forging a new curriculum for a rural high school, therefore, school personnel may need to take several factors into account before, while, and after doing so: the consolidated or autonomous nature of their school system; the moral structures in place within the community; consideration of outcomes and activities that will benefit students of the locale, whether or not they decide to later leave the area; an existing curriculum that is likely to be rigid and long-standing; the availability of financial and human resources; and finally, their own biases and wishes.   These variables, among others, will affect the process of curriculum-making in the rural high school, causing deliberation and decision-making on the matter to be a potentially delicate and painstaking task.   Furthermore, the shared decision-making necessary for complete curricular discussion in a small school may or may not be present, depending on the willingness of each faculty member to participate.

In the final portion of this book, a contemporary, real-life case study of a rural high school will be examined, as the faculty of the school struggles to engage itself in a meaningful curricular dialogue for the improvement of its instruction.   Coming into play, the reader will note, are a large number of the various social, historical, and philosophical factors related to rural education previously discussed.

8. Rural Curriculum in Neosho, Indiana

The weeds are high where corn don't grow.

– Travis Tritt

In an effort to further illustrate the mechanics of modern curriculum-making in the rural school, the author conducted a year-long study of a high school where many of the furies of contemporary rural curriculum were imploding together. The high school examined was considering a comprehensive reform of its curriculum, and the author sought to ascertain components that teachers wished to see included and excluded in a new document (if a formal document was to be created). In addition, the author collected teacher and administrator responses regarding their perceived ability to change or continue the curriculum in response to state and local expectations. It is assumed that this study may provide a benchmark of themes from which future examinations of rural curriculum may develop.

In light of the fact that only one rural community was examined, the conclusions found in this study cannot be generalized to all rural high schools. As with most forms of qualitative research, the generalizability of the findings is limited; and has been already explained in this book, it is a mistake to generalize the characteristics of any group of schools. It is the hope of the author, nonetheless, that the findings shed light on the qualities of high schools in rural America which may be common while simultaneously displaying how differences might also emerge in other places.

Neosho, the site involved in this study, is located in southern Indiana. Approximately forty miles from both a major city and research university, the consolidated school corporation includes an area of 64.1 square miles, thus including other townships outside the Neosho community.

A Baptist church appeared in the area in 1840, but its parishioners did not reside in the community. The village of Neosho was founded in 1855 by a single pioneer who purchased twenty lots. The town soon became a settling point for a variety of artisans and craftsmen. Initially, a grist mill provided most of the employment for those without a trade skill; soon after, however, a sawmill also appeared to enhance the economy of the area. A raging fire destroyed almost the entire town in 1878, but the remaining citizens quickly recovered to build another community in its image. Blanchard (1884) noted the unique quality of the town, with its thriving businesses:

> There is not a livelier town of its size [350 persons at the time] in the county. This is accounted for by reason of the location of the village in the center of a rich tract of country, and its distance from railroad towns and the enterprise of the citizens. (p. 146)

Blanchard (1884) also recounts the early history of Neosho schools in this fashion:

> It is stated that the first school held in the township was in [Neosho], in about the year 1835. A rude log cabin that had been occupied a short time by some early family and had then been vacated, was fitted up, and a school was taught [sic] by some stranger, probably an Irishman, who came along. A school was taught soon afterward in the northern part of the township, the Wheelers being the principal patrons. It is said that one of them was the teacher. This school was taught about the year 1836. Another was taught east of it within a year or two afterward. In 1840, there were four established schools, two in the northern part of the township, one near the

center, and one near Neosho, or near what afterward became Neosho. The real development of the school system of the township began with the passage of the common school law of 1852. Frame houses were built, and public funds provided better wages for teachers, and thus secured better instructors. Now there are eight or nine schools in the township, and the value of the school property is about $5,500. (p. 144)

The current schoolhouse for the community was built in 1907, and with the exception of modest renovation projects in 1916 and 1957, has remained virtually unchanged. Nine years after construction, a sum of $5,732 was contracted for remodeling – most of which was used to complete the basement left unfinished by the original work. In 1927, a new gymnasium was built onto the existing structure, and reflected the community's interest in extracurricular activities, particularly basketball.

The 1970 census showed Neosho as being nearly half as large as it had been one hundred years ago, with a population of 200. Nonetheless, there was still evidence of artisans and full-time craftsmen in the area that year. Identified in town at this time were two druggists, two shoe and bootmakers, four carpenters, a tinner, and three blacksmiths. However, without extensive employment opportunities within the town, many residents of Neosho commute to the large nearby city for work.

The enrollment of Neosho High School (grades 7-12) had remained fairly constant from 1988 to 1998, as seen below:

Enrollment at Neosho High School, 1987-1997

Year	Total Enrollment
1987-88	222
1988-89	209
1989-90	242
1990-91	241
1991-92	194
1992-93	204
1993-94	201
1994-95	223
1995-96	226
1996-97	237

(Indiana Department of Education, 1998)

What has experienced great fluctuation during this period, however, is the percentage of Neosho High School graduates going on to college. In 1996, 45% of the graduates pursued higher education, as compared to 19% of the 1995 class; from the class of 1994, 28% of the students continued their education after high school. Nineteen full-time teachers were employed at Neosho High in 1997, with an average age of 37 years, and seven years of teaching experience. Eleven of the full-time teachers held bachelor's degrees, while the remaining eight had attained master's degrees. The high school maintained a 12.2:1 student/teacher ratio, while the state average rested at 17.9:1.

Thirty-four percent of the graduating seniors in 1997 took the Scholastic Aptitude Test (SAT), which trailed the state average of 52%, and was well below the 1996 class at Neosho High School of 53%; the percentage of seniors at the high school taking the American College Test (ACT) also trailed the state average (4.5% to 17.3%). However, the average *scores* on the SAT (1014 to 991) and ACT (25.5 to 21.1) for students at the high school were above the state average. During the 1996-97 school year there were no student suspensions or expulsions for weapon, drug, or alcohol offenses, as opposed to a 2.5% rate for other high schools throughout Indiana (IDE, 1998).

Methodological Underpinnings of the Study

Conducted as a naturalistic case study, this investigation involved the author in an examination of a single school within its contextual setting. Schwandt (1997) notes that "naturalistic inquiry" has been defined as "the investigation of phenomena within and in relation to their naturally occurring contexts" (p. 101). Borg and Gall (1989) describe a case study as involving "an investigator who makes a detailed examination of a single subject or group or phenomenon" (p. 402). In utilizing a case-study method for this inquiry, the author hoped to develop a broad, complete picture of the dialogue transpiring within a small, rural high school staff in regard to its curriculum. In this realm, many theories exist for the retrieval, organization, and presentation of data in qualitative inquiry. In pursuit of these theories, Wolcott (1994) asks, "How do qualitatively oriented authors 'transform' what they see and hear into intelligible accounts?" (p. 1) Certainly, the presentation of a valid, organized, and worthwhile qualitative inquiry can assume a variety of forms and structures. As "post-postivistic" or "non-scientific" as the work may sometimes seem, however, the qualitative author must nonetheless organize his data into what becomes an orderly account of a culture.

In a somewhat contradicting tone, Jackson (1990) encourages qualitative authors to view their environments in an open, non-judgmental framework; while it is important to be organized in retrieving data, the author must be cognizant of the variety of aspects to consider in ethnographic studies.

> Perhaps the idea of looking *for* something in educational research is what is wrong. Perhaps we have become so intent in looking *for* that we no longer know how to look *at*. Perhaps looking *for* encourages us to look *past* things rather than at them. Looking *for* constricts awareness; looking *at* expands it. (p. 163).

Thus, the job of the qualitative author can become one of maintaining a delicate balance of telling an engaging story while maintaining the structure of organized research. Jackson asserts that it is crucial for the author to keep an "open eye" to all components of qualitative data-gathering. In order to organize these components into a worthwhile, valid study, the author may involve the process of "triangulation," as defined by Schwandt (1997):

> [Triangulation] is a procedure used to establish the fact that the criterion of *validity* has been met. The fieldworker makes inferences from the data, claiming that a particular set of data supports a particular definition, theme, assertion, hypothesis, claim, etc. Triangulation is a means of checking the integrity of the inferences one draws. It can involve the use of multiple data sources, multiple investigators, multiple theoretical perspectives, multiple methods, or all of these. The central point of the procedure is to examine a single social phenomenon from more than one vantage point. (p. 163)

As contextualized with Schwandt's definition, the purpose of triangulation in this study was to help authenticate the "curricular intentions" of the teaching staff; in other words, to make certain that responses given in interview sessions matched (at least, to a reasonable extent) teacher practices in regard to curriculum. To make matters more complex, however, the idea of triangulation is altered by the subjectivity of the author. The interpretation of messages and gestures at faculty meetings, for instance, played a large role in shaping the author's views on curriculum development within the staff; what the author witnessed as "hostile" discussion between two faculty members on a given subject may actually be the normal tone of conversation expected. The qualitative author always strives (in vain, perhaps) for a balance between objectivity and subjectivity as well; while personality and perspective will always rear its head, the author also pursues a position of neutral observation, a disinterested third party who seeks to decipher data in an accurate and just manner. This balance was precisely the pursuit of the author in this study.

Sample

The entire full-time teaching staff at Neosho High School was asked to complete an initial questionnaire, which enlisted their participation in follow-up interviews. From this instrument, the author not only learned the demographic make-up of the staff but also those who have had prior experience with curriculum development and revision. With the full-time teaching staff encompassing nineteen individuals, a sufficient number of respondents was expected. Neosho High School was selected for this study, in part, because of this low number of faculty; in such a circumstance, it is possible for the author to gain a thorough understanding of the curricular perspectives of the entire teaching force. Upon reviewing the questionnaires, the author found that eighteen of the nineteen teachers (95%) agreed to take part in the interviews. While not taking part in formal interview sessions, the high school principal in this study engaged in intermittent conversations with the author, offering various perspectives on the curricular climate of the school (as will be shown in subsequent chapters).

Instrumentation

After the initial questionnaire was distributed among school personnel, the author gained a better understanding of the demographics of the school staff. With the study being conducted in a naturalistic sense, however, the author himself comprised the primary instrument for this study. The author observed the classrooms of various subject areas and grade levels, sat in on school board meetings, studied the lesson plans of teachers, and considered other forces that propelled the formation and execution of the curriculum. In addition to interviewing each teacher in two thirty-minute sessions (with two selected individuals participating in three sessions, and another completing only one), the author also observed two fifty-minute class sessions of each teacher in the high school, along with examining the lesson plans and encompassing unit plans of the particular class sessions. These observations were conducted to witness content examples of each of the teacher's courses, as well as to notice any efforts towards inter-disciplinary work between teachers of different departments occurring at the time of observation.

In each classroom observation, the author sat in the back of the room, typically facing the teacher and the backs of students. The author was not directly involved in any classroom activities, although his input was engaged in one class discussion regarding current news issues. Prior to witnessing the class sessions, the author studied the lesson plan for the given day as well as the objectives and accomplishments of the previous class meeting.

As agreed before commencing the interviews, none of the interview sessions went longer than thirty minutes. Each session lasted a minimum of twenty-five minutes, with the exception of one nineteen-minute conversation. Although questions were structured beforehand, respondents in the interviews were encouraged to be informal, so as to engage in a relaxed dialogue. Certain questions called for specific, short responses; however, the open-ended nature of most questions provided extensive insight into perceptions of the curriculum and the process of curriculum development in the high school.

Data Collection

Early in the study, the author attempted to schedule regular visits to the school on particular days. However, due to scheduling difficulties on the part of the author and the high school staff, the visits ultimately occurred on a varied schedule, as the author contacted the informants by telephone to set interview times that accommodated each other's schedules. Visits by the author and examination of the existing curriculum was limited to the junior and senior high school (grades 7-12) and did not extend to the elementary schools.

The number of interviews that took place with each informant was not pre-determined, but sufficient data was gathered after two sessions with each individual. Third interview sessions took place with Steve, a social studies teacher, and Dante, a language arts teacher, to clarify data given in previous sessions. Wilma, another language arts teacher, chose to complete only one session. The questions listed below were used in interviews with each respondent.

Interview Questions

1) Do you think that the school changing from a consolidated system to a "community" system will affect the curriculum? Why or why not?

2) How closely, do you feel, does your course textbook follow the community-sanctioned curriculum?

3) Do you think your subject area is a valued portion of the curriculum, in the eyes of the community? Of other teachers? Of your students? Why or why not?

4) In what ways does the curriculum of this school reflect the values of the community?

5) Where did the current curriculum for your classes come from?

6) How are curriculum decisions usually made in your school?

7) Have you ever experienced pressure or suggestions to change the curriculum? In what manner? By whom?

8) What would you like to see included in a new curriculum for this high school?

9) Are you aware of the components of the state-mandated curriculum? (If the answer is "no," a copy of the state-mandated curriculum will be provided for the respondent's review)

10) Which of these components should be continued as required items? Why?

The interview sessions were audiotaped. In addition to transcribing the responses, the author also logged gestures and expressions displayed during the interviews. Upon completing the transcriptions, the tapes were destroyed. The interviews typically took place in the teachers' classrooms during preparatory or lunch periods to ensure privacy. If such a room was unavailable, the "Teacher Work Room" was utilized, a small lounge area in which other faculty members gave the author and respondent temporary privacy. With all interview data, pseudonyms (approved by the respondents) were used in the write-up of the data to protect the confidentiality of the informants. Upon transcribing the interviews, the author provided copies of the transcript for review by the respondents. The author asked the respondents to make any necessary corrections, additions, or deletions to their testimony on the transcript, and return it to the author. The corrected copies would then become the data for the final write-up. Of the eighteen teachers that participated in the interviews, one returned a corrected transcript to the author. If no corrections, additions, or deletions were seen as necessary by the respondent, he or she was invited to retain the transcript.

Several types of documents were reviewed by the author. These documents included parent, teacher, and student guides to the high school; school newsletters; student newspapers and publications; various assignments and course syllabi given by teachers within the classrooms; lesson and unit plans of the individual teachers; course textbooks; and information on the mandated curricular subjects of the state of Indiana. The author looked to these documents to provide insight into the curricular structure of the high school. During the review of these documents, the author was asked by the members of one particular academic department to participate in their selection of a textbook for the following year. The author declined this invitation, as it was seen as a conflict of interest in the course of this study.

In addition to conducting interviews and reviewing documents, the author also carried out extensive observations of multiple facets of the school environment. These observations included classrooms within the high school, departmental and general faculty meetings, and school board meetings. Field notes were taken during the classroom and faculty meeting observations, while the author audiotaped school board meetings (upon transcription, these tapes were also destroyed). In compiling the field notes, the author specifically logged the pedagogical interactions between the teachers and students, such as the introduction of new material, establishment of lesson objectives, guided practice, and so forth. This was done to ascertain congruence between the intended strategies of the lesson plan and its execution. Relatively few notes were written by the author at the various scenes; rather, most of the data were compiled after each class session, as the author focused on the "sights and sounds" of the teaching-and-learning process during the instructional periods.

In all of the observation settings, it was hoped that the involvement of the author would be of the least-invasive manner, so as not to interfere with planned activities, and also to provide valid data to be compiled by having the informants act as "naturally" as possible.

Data Analysis

Upon the completion of the interview sessions, classroom and school board/faculty meeting observations, and the review of pertinent documents, the author began the process of analyzing the multitude of data on curriculum discourse that was collected. After the analysis process (as described below), the author constructed themes from the data, or "patterned regularities," as Wolcott (1994, p. 33) calls them. Themes are the dominant patterns of behavior in the study, whose details were embedded in the data that were extracted and organized by the author. The themes that emerged in this inquiry will be discussed in the final chapters.

As mentioned previously, a variety of strategies have been used by authors for the analysis of qualitative data. Wolcott (1994) recommends a general ten-step process for such analyses, and this process was utilized by the author for the analysis of data in this study.

The first two steps involved the highlighting and display of the findings. Upon reading the interview transcripts and reflecting upon field notes several times, the author made note cards for potential thematic areas. The "display," as Wolcott calls it, involves the physical placement of the data before the author. This idea suggests that "graphic presentation offers an alternative not only for conveying information but for dramatizing or emphasizing particular aspects of a study" (p. 31). When physically present before him, the wealth of qualitative data was more easily organized by the author.

The third and fourth steps required the author to maintain, and then "flesh out," systematic fieldwork procedures and analytical frameworks (pp. 32-33). This is where the "non-scientific" qualitative author seeks to be *more* scientific, establishing and following a pattern of regular field inquiry strategies. In this study, the themes were being built by the author as the process of investigation was unfolding. For example, the perspectives of one teacher in an interview, unknowingly, served as a framework or "backdrop" to those of the next. The observation of teachers' classrooms and lesson plans reinforced or contradicted the responses given in the interview sessions, thus helping to give a broader and more complex account as the study continued.

In the fifth step of Wolcott's strategy, the "patterned regularities" (themes) are more clearly identified. As suggested by the above sequence, themes may be constructed by the author as the study progresses and not necessarily as an end-product only. This idea is supported by Biklen and Bogden (1982), as some authors construct themes as the study simultaneously evolves:

> It is useful to think of approaches to analysis falling into two modes. One is an approach where analysis is concurrent with data collection and is more or less completed by the time the data is gathered. This practice is more commonly practiced by experienced fieldworkers. If you know what you are doing it is most efficient and effective. The other mode involves collecting data before doing the analysis. Because reflecting about what you are finding while in the field is part of every qualitative study, authors only approach this mode, never following it in its pure form. (p. 146)

Thus, the author found both revelation and accuracy in noting possible themes *during* data collection, each of which accumulated or lost strength as the study continued.

In steps six, seven, and eight, Wolcott suggests the comparison of the case study with one or more that are similar as a method of quality control (p. 33), and the subsequent contextualization of the study in a broader analytical framework. In following this process, the author referred back to case studies noted in review of the relevant literature, and reflected on the similarities and differences to better contextualize the characteristics of the curricular culture at Neosho High School. As this process unfolded, the author noticed several patterns of behavior in other cases similar to those found at Neosho, as well as some that were different. This assisted the author in considering the relative generalizability of the Neosho curricular situation to schools similar in size and structure.

Finally, Wolcott suggests that the author critique the inquiry process, and propose a re-design for the case study. This idea will be covered in the final chapter, as the author unveils the implications of this study for future research.

The Teaching Staff at Neosho High School

As mentioned, eighteen of the nineteen full-time teachers at Neosho High School agreed to participate in the interview process for this study. They were identified in the study with the following pseudonyms:

- Rudy, in the industrial arts department, with 10 years of teaching experience
- Wilma, language arts, 16 years
- Cindy, foreign languages, 9 years
- Dante, language arts, 2 years
- Renee, physical education, first year
- Delila, art, 9 years
- Steve, social studies, 4 years
- Monica, special education, 7 years
- Mary, home economics, 23 years
- Reba, mathematics, 2 years
- Dave, chorus and band, first year
- Isaiah, language arts, 1 year
- George, social studies, 23 years
- Kathy, science, first year
- Mickey, science, first year
- Susan, agricultural education, first year
- Betty, physical education, first year
- Jack, mathematics, 1 year

The responses of the principal ("Dr. Allen") were not audiotaped. The author often spoke with the principal in a harried setting (walking in the hallway, in between the principal's other responsibilities, etc.), and thus it was agreed that taping of his comments would be impractical. Furthermore, the focus of this study was on the teachers' perspectives of curriculum-making; the author sought to somewhat "circumvent" the principal in this regard, and both he and the principal wished to have the teachers respond to interview questions unconcerned about the principal's reaction to their feelings.

The interviews for this study were completed between January and May, 1998. The compilation, organization, and presentation of all the data was completed by December, 1998.

9. The Curricular Discourse at Neosho High School

One man with courage is a majority.

– Thomas Jefferson

During the 1997-98 school year, Neosho High School held the distinction of being one of the smallest public high schools in the state of Indiana (in terms of enrollment), as well as having *the* lowest-paid faculty in the state. These two factors, among several others, impacted the ability and willingness of staff members to re-conceptualize the curriculum of the school.

In considering the small staff size at Neosho, the school appeared to be an adequate physical structure in which to teach – despite what a couple of the teachers had described as "cramped conditions." The building, while not large, appeared to the author to have ample space for teacher and student work. Outside of the actual classrooms, however, there was an evident lack of private space for lunch, meetings, and other non-teaching activities throughout the day. Although some teachers were forced to share classrooms, most had their own rooms, and these were personalized to their particular interests and subjects. Since the high school and the elementary school shared one gymnasium, the physical education teachers were particularly concerned about the lack of space for their programs.

The changing face of the Neosho community introduced a new challenge to the issue of available space in the high school. A new wave of residential areas was beginning to appear within the Neosho limits, and their occupants were primarily composed of individuals who worked corporate jobs at the major city forty miles away (according to the school staff). It was apparent that many of these people were leaving the immediate city area and looking to purchase housing in smaller communities surrounding the metropolitan region – such as in Neosho. The result had been a steady (though relatively small) growth in population for communities like Neosho which consequently was placing a strain on the antiquated school facilities in such towns. The high school building in Neosho, as in other small towns in Indiana, has remained in use for many decades. These small-town high school buildings were not designed to hold ever-increasing numbers of students, but rather a consistent, year-to-year, "controllable" figure. Thus, communities like Neosho have been suddenly forced to deal with issues of new construction for schools. However, before this issue could be addressed for the *future*, the school system needed to find a way to provide adequate facilities for its students in the current year. Two temporary "trailers" were set up for the 1997-98 school year in an effort to partially alleviate overcrowding.

The teachers themselves, however, were not among those choosing to call the Neosho community home. Rather, it was apparent to the author that most of the teachers lived a good distance from the school. One of the math teachers lived 45 miles away, another teacher 39 miles, and several others 40 miles away in the large city within the region. Only two teachers – interestingly, two of the teachers with the longest tenures on the staff – lived within the Neosho school district limits. As young teachers dominated the ranks of the faculty, they made it clear that the town of Neosho offered little for their personal lives.

The lack of teachers living within the district posed an interesting question in the mind of the author. Was the teachers' withdrawal from the area a sign of disinterest for the future success of the school? During their interviews, many teachers conveyed a concern for the next generation of Neosho students, notwithstanding the fact that they lived elsewhere. Many appeared to be deeply committed to their jobs and expressed a genuine empathy for their students. However, as teachers displayed an overwhelming tendency to live in other communities, this attitude communicated a significant lack of long-term dedication to the school system. As will be discussed later, several teachers were planning to leave their jobs at the end of 1997-98 school year; they sought more lucrative teaching jobs in the cities and larger towns that they called home.

In addition to the low pay, other factors appeared to contribute to an unfavorable working environment for many Neosho High School teachers. Most prominently, teachers sensed a very paternalistic attitude resonating from the administration and school board. Some younger teachers in particular suggested that the school board misunderstood them as professionals and discouraged innovative, new teaching techniques recently acquired in their teacher education experiences. The little interest that the board expressed in their day-to-day teaching, they noted, only sought to maintain extremely traditional pedagogical practices that were considered "outdated" by the teachers. However, almost all teachers – young and old – were frustrated by certain "traditions" in the general work environment. For example, an interesting aspect of the building was a bell that relieved the teachers at the end of their contracted workday. Many of the teachers lined up at the door at 3:45 in the afternoon, waiting for this bell. This was atypical of the informal, pleasant reputation of the small rural school, as noted earlier by Leight and Rinehart (1992). Rather, this treatment was a strong indicator of individuals looking to leave their jobs (both on a daily *and* permanent basis) as quickly as possible.

Thus, the author sensed a feeling of "temporary employment" throughout the building; this was significant when one considers that the teachers were asked to reconstruct the current curriculum for the school. It might be assumed that most teachers (not just at Neosho, but most any school) would like to see their efforts in curricular reform last at least a few years, so that their carefully-devised changes will take effect. However, as in the case of the Neosho High School teachers, the question must be asked: how confident can the students, administration, community, and other teachers be in a curriculum developed mostly by teachers who do not plan to be at the school for very long?

Furthermore, the idea of "temporary employment" was not unique to the teaching staff. In the past two decades, Neosho High

School has employed eight different principals and eight different superintendents. The teachers that weathered the frequent changes in administration had grown weary of the new prompts for curricular dialogue that seemed to arrive automatically with each new leadership group. In keeping form, the principal that initiated this curriculum dialogue for the faculty – Dr. Allen – would leave his position at the end of the 1997-98 school year. Several faculty members had truly felt that "things would be different" under Dr. Allen; he appeared to many of the teachers to be extremely dedicated to the Neosho school system. Nonetheless, he remained in his position for one academic year and accepted another administrative position in a school system not far from Neosho. When giving reasons for his departure, Dr. Allen primarily expressed frustration with a school board that was inflexible.

Seeking greater alignment within subject areas, as well as better communication links with the elementary school, the administration at Neosho High School prompted the staff to commence a study of the school's curricular efforts in the fall of 1997. The completion of this discussion was left open-ended, but reasonable, regular progress was expected towards the aforementioned goals. The idea was initially presented to the teachers in a staff meeting in October, during which the faculty was asked to reconsider what was taught in the classrooms, how much time was spent on each unit that was taught, and how grade-to-grade transfer of student work could become more helpful and meaningful – not only to the students, but also to teachers, administrators, and local citizens.

As mentioned previously, a new superintendent and high school principal arrived at Neosho for the 1997-98 school year. Although the elementary school was located in the same building, a separate office existed for the high school. The high school office housed not only the principal but also the superintendent of the Neosho Consolidated School Corporation which changed to "Neosho Community Schools" on January 1, 1998. Despite the fact that the principal of the high school and the superintendent were new for the 1997-98 year, the staff had actually become accustomed to change in this area, as noted by one veteran teacher.

> Dr. Allen is the eighth principal I've worked for here, and
> Mr. Simmons is the eighth superintendent. They come, and

they go; the administration is a revolving door. And simple division tells you how long they stay – less than three years.

The high turnover rate among principals and superintendents remained a strong issue related to curriculum development and reform at the high school. Most staff members were not confident that any given administrative team at the high school would remain long enough to ensure that benefits would ultimately evolve from reform projects; 16 out of the 19 teachers believed that they would work under another principal during their stay at Neosho. Several teachers were extremely wary of new administrators – not in a personal sense, but out of a concern that a new curricular "fad" would be thrust upon them. They were fearful of comprehensive, systemic change in the image of the new person(s) in charge and believed that this process was virtually inevitable with the arrival of new leadership.

This attitude notwithstanding, it was evident that the majority of the staff was personally fond of the new principal and superintendent and spoke highly of most of their efforts to make the school a better place to work. The principal was frequently seen in the hallways and classrooms, visiting with students and staff while listening to, and showing concern for, their problems. At times, the principal even filled in as a substitute teacher when no other replacement could be found. One could argue that this scenario is typical of the small-town school with limited human resources, but it appeared, in this case, to be the result of the gracious nature of a caring individual. When compared with past administrators, one teacher described Dr. Allen as "more insightful, more efficient, and better educated."

Existence of a Current Curriculum Document

Efforts in the past to develop a formal, structured curriculum resulted in an uncertain product. More than half of the current full-time teachers (11 out of 19) were unsure if a written, school board-approved curricular document actually existed at the school. "I know that they worked on it a couple of years ago for the state," a younger staff member observed. "But no, I've never seen one [a formal written curriculum] for my subject area." Of the eight that believed one did exist, the responses varied as to what it actually comprised.

Some teachers believed that the formal curriculum was the outcome of the Performance-Based Assessment (PBA) review that took place at the school in 1995. Other teachers in specific subject areas (especially in Art and Industrial/Agricultural Education) viewed the current curriculum, for their purposes, to be not what the school system *as a whole* agreed upon, but rather what they had developed themselves – either in a short time, or over a period of several years. Furthermore, a few younger teachers believed their curriculum to be the textbook that was left for them, since they were hired shortly before the school year began.

While sitting in the principal's office, the author asked Dr. Allen if he, in his short time at the high school, had himself discovered a formal, written curriculum. He indicated that he had not, while directing attention to the numerous file cabinets that loomed behind his desk. He stated that the results of numerous prior curricular reform efforts lay within these files. It was his intention to review all of the files and see if they could somehow provide a starting point for beginning the process again in a practical, efficient manner.

Requirements for Graduation from Neosho High School

Within public high schools in the United States, the graduation requirements for students are typically congruent with the formal curriculum, providing in segmented form a broader overview of the curricular path the students will travel. Requirements for graduation are significant to the study of the greater school operation, for they might convey local cultural values, the general educational values of the school system, and the desired "end product" for an educated young person in the given community (Peshkin, 1978).

The requirements for graduation from Neosho High School include the following:

- Candidates for graduation must have earned a minimum of 40 credits (one credit equals one semester).

- Students must meet the 8-semester attendance requirement and be enrolled as a full-time student during each of those semesters.

- Earning enough credits does not guarantee that a student will graduate. The student must be recommended for graduation by the principal.

Students have the option of earning the regular high school diploma. Requirements for this diploma are listed in the appendix; at first glance at those lists, one might consider this to be a wide range of course selections for the students at Neosho. This list of possibilities, however, may be reduced until the first day of classes in August. With fewer students compared to their typical urban and suburban counterparts, the curricular offerings of many smaller rural high schools (such as Neosho) are sometimes dependent upon sufficient enrollment. Courses that are typically considered "electives" might not be available at such a setting, as in certain foreign languages, the arts, etc. Furthermore, advanced core courses that may be required for college entrance (such as Calculus, Trigonometry, Advanced Placement Physics, and others) might not be offered; nor does the school have distance learning technologies that would enable students to participate in courses offered at other sites. Students may *view* courses taught at other sites, but not directly participate in them. Even this option, however, is unreliable. "The satellite doesn't always work," said one teacher who was skeptical of the process.

Hence, it is not incorrect to assume that the Neosho students' potential post-secondary educational experiences are negatively altered by their school's small size. In fact, one teacher's daughter may not be able to take the advanced physics course for this reason (as shown in the appendix, only two students registered for the course during the 1996-97 year). She displays her concern with an uncertain feeling about the future.

I've got a daughter here, she's a junior, she's going to be a senior next year, and I'm really concerned about the courses she's going to be able to take – is she going to be able to take Physics? She's due for it next year. Now, it's given over the TV; and they're going to make some cuts. I just hope it's not going to be in areas that are really important. I'm sure they're going to look at Physics and say, "Well, how many students are going to take Physics?" And we do have a teacher here who I think is capable of teaching it, and I know that they're going to make cuts in classes that have only two or three students. We need to build, we need new classrooms, this place is growing – and we need to grow with it. I think there's only one student this year taking Physics over the TV.

By "taking it over the TV," the teacher is referring to the older, simpler process of the student only viewing the course material on the television – not interacting with others involved with the course at different locations, in the modern sense of the term "distance education." This teacher is one of only two on the staff who lives within the district boundaries of Neosho; consequently, she may have a greater stake in the formation of any new curriculum, as her children are involved as learners in the system. Another teacher is pursuing grant money for distance education capabilities for the school, but it may be a period of several years before this idea becomes a reality.

Expectations for Growth and the Expansion of the Curriculum
Although current prospects for the curriculum are limited, it is not an entirely hopeless situation for the future of Neosho and its schools. Despite its diminutive size and relative lack of industrial opportunity, the town has recently experienced, and expects to maintain, a pattern of slight population growth. The high school (including grades 7-12) enrollment for the 1997-98 school year was 238, as compared with the projected figure of 275 by the year 2000 (IDE, 1998). Without being aware of these published figures, the faculty nonetheless appeared cognizant of the possibility for future growth and understood the implications for the expansion of the curriculum. Betty, a physical education teacher at the high school, however, saw the growth as being incompatible with the current facilities for her subject area, and consequently she foresaw a curricular difficulty.

> We have to grow – the community is growing, leaps and bounds. Being a Physical Education teacher, the way I look at it, we need another gym. There are a lot of things that the elementary kids are missing out on; after-school programs, etc.

Others seemed unconcerned about the increasing population; the situation was seen as an opportunity for expansion, rather than a cause for alarm. "Supposedly, there was a feasibility study done," noted Isaiah, an English teacher, "and by the year 2003, somewhere in that five-year span, there will be between 700-800 kids here [in the entire K-12 system]." Jack, a teacher in the math department, cited similar figures. "I know we've had projections that [Neosho] is supposed to grow. In the next five to ten years, we're supposed to get up to around a thousand kids." Again, many were encouraged by this upswing; others worried about available space, or ability to add on buildings to the existing structure.

Despite this split in considering the physical ramifications of growth, a general consensus was seen in regard to the future of the curriculum. With the enrollment figures expected to continue increasing, most staff members understood the importance of enhancing and expanding the curriculum of the high school; expanding not only to offer *more* courses, but simply to *provide* courses that other schools might consider routine components of their curricula. As discussed by Church (1988), teachers can possess and execute tremendous power when it comes to curricular production and when given authority by the school administration to do so. However, the participants must be willing, active "change agents" to initiate this production. For, as was shown in case studies similar to Neosho (Kannapel, et al., 1995; Bachus, 1992; McCracken & Miller, 1988), producing curriculum is often an unwanted (though necessary) extra task assumed by teachers. Many of the teachers at Neosho were simply not interested in discussions on curriculum, despite the important ramifications of those discussions.

On the other hand, some teachers were concerned that some key academic areas may even be cut due to low enrollment. And, as one may infer from comparing the enrollment figures within individual courses and the requirements for college admission presented earlier, these cuts may include higher-level courses that are critical for students who wish to advance to post-secondary education. Courses such as Advanced Physics and Calculus may be offered from another site through television, but even the status of this remained uncertain for the future as the 1997-98 school year continued.

Curriculum Mandated by the State

Public Law 20-10.1-4-1-15 of the Indiana Code provides a "mandated curriculum" for the schools in the state. This law stipulates guidelines for the instruction of particular content and skills, as noted below:

Topics Mandated for Instruction by the State of Indiana
• Indiana and United States Constitutions
• The availability of certain writings in each school's library or media center, and the right to post these writings, including:
  - The Constitution of the United States of America
  - The National Motto
  - The National Anthem
  - The Pledge of Allegiance
  - The Constitution of the State of Indiana
  - The Declaration of Independence
  - The Mayflower Compact
  - The Federalist Papers
  - "Common Sense" by Thomas Paine
  - The writings, speeches, documents, and proclamations of the founding fathers and presidents of the United States
  - United States Supreme Court decisions
  - Executive orders of presidents of the United States
  - Frederick Douglass' Speech at Rochester, New York on July 5, 1852, entitled "What to a Slave is the Fourth of July?"
  - *Appeal* by David Walker
  - Chief Seattle's letter to the United States government in 1852 in response to the United States government's inquiry regarding the purchase of tribal lands

• History of the American system of government
• Morals instruction (honesty, courtesy, obedience to law, respect for the national flag, etc.)
• Good citizenship instruction (respecting authority, others, property of others, one's self, etc.)

- A school corporation curriculum (including language arts, mathematics, social studies, sciences, fine arts / music, health / physical fitness, etc.)
- Safety education
- Hygienic education (student may be excused if in conflict with religious beliefs)
- Prevention of disease spread by rats, flies, and mosquitoes
- Illicit drugs / establishment of drug-free communities
- Acquired Immune Deficiency Syndrome (AIDS) education
- Human sexuality education
- Career development education
- Breast cancer / testicular cancer education
- Blood donor / human organ donor education
(Indiana General Assembly, 1998)

The majority of the items listed above relate to the subject areas of health and social studies; in terms of standards for math and language arts, the state's recommendations mirrored those made by the National Council of Teachers of English (NCTE) and the National Council of Teachers of Mathematics (NCTM). As part of the interview process, teachers in the areas of health and social studies were asked their knowledge of the various state curricular components. Few knew of their existence as law, much less what they comprised. This, perhaps, is symptomatic of a larger communicative scenario: the inability of the state to oversee the execution of educational legislation. Although no teachers specifically addressed communication difficulties with the state as problematic, there was nonetheless a certain amount of concern about the ever-increasing requirements that larger legislative bodies (such as the state government) were heaping on the public schools. In various ways, several teachers cited the phrase that "responsibilities are always added to teachers' jobs, and none are ever taken away." With a small staff and limited resources, many teachers at Neosho felt overburdened with their responsibilities *as they stood* and cringed when the idea of a "state mandated curriculum" was considered – as if other new components would soon be added to their jobs.

The concept of curricular components promulgated at the state level, therefore, was unknown by some staff members. As seen in Chapter Three, the state is often unable to oversee the curricular operations of individual schools. Most of the teachers at Neosho, however, were unconcerned about either the state or the local school administration discovering the presence (or lack thereof) of the mandates in their teaching. "The state of Indiana will never know what I teach inside the four walls of my classroom," one teacher noted, "and they never will know."

The Community and the Curriculum
     Despite the relatively small size of the Neosho community, the faculty sensed an extreme disjuncture between the citizens and the day-to-day operations of the school, particularly as related to curricular issues. A small newsletter is available monthly during the school year, but the town appears to be otherwise disengaged from what transpires within school board, faculty, and administrative meetings about curriculum. This was noted by Steve, one of the social studies teachers.

> I think the community has a lukewarm feeling towards education. Now certainly, there are some families within the community which that would not be true of; either they don't care at all, or they care greatly. But I think, community-wide, the average Joe that drives by the high school, on any day, is very lukewarm to what takes place here. They're not aware of what takes place, and some of that's our fault. They don't care about it, and I think that's systemic to the community.

     Another teacher estimated that as much as 70% of the local economy is farming-based and that this may also contribute to the relative disinterest of citizens about school and curricular matters. Mickey, a faculty member in the science department added, "I have six kids in my Earth Science class, and of the six, four of them *are* farmers." Furthermore, the physical placement of the school may cause apathy as well. There is little business activity in the part of town where the high school lies; despite being on a state highway, the high school is neighbored only by a bank, video store, post office, and church, along with several abandoned or otherwise empty buildings. Most of the residential areas of Neosho are situated a considerable distance from the high school, which may alter the willingness of community members not only to visit the school, but also attend important events such as school board meetings and conferences with faculty and administration. Isaiah believed whole-heartedly that the agrarian nature of the town contributed to the inert nature of its curriculum, but that there was possibility for growth or revision even in the traditional "subject area" of agriculture.

> The stereotypical kid here is the farmer kid who's going to get out of school, and go back and work on the farm. And so, if you base an answer on that, no, English is not that important. They can talk, but they're not going to do a whole lot of writing, or a lot of communicating with someone other than a farmer... the farming industry has probably changed from 50 years ago, and it will continue to change. So, it takes a certain degree of intellectual ability to keep up with those changes. I think it's valued in that aspect; I don't think the community would really care if they knew who Dante was, or diagram a sentence as long they had the fundamental areas down.

Thus, for a variety of possible reasons (but yet in contrast to the "typical" rural school, as discussed earlier), little interaction appeared to exist between the township and the school system. This remained a concern for teachers, particularly as to how the curriculum was perceived in the locality. Jack, in the math department, bluntly appraised the situation. "I'm not sure how many of the people in the community actually know what goes on here, and what doesn't go on. I would be concerned if a teacher walked in and was able to teach just anything." Upon further consideration, Steve thought favorably of the possibility of the community being aware of the school's operations. "There might actually be an outcry if someone ever found out what we're actually doing in here," he offered. After pausing to reflect, however, he continued. "On the other hand, we might win an award."

Initial Staff Meeting on Curriculum
As the idea of curriculum revision was considered by the school administration, a staff meeting (involving all of the full-time teachers) was held in November, 1997 to engage in preliminary dialogue on the matter. The meeting was held in the school library (the closest thing to a "conference room" that the school possessed), and took place after a regular school day for approximately forty-five minutes. The principal, Dr. Allen, opened the discussion by pointing

to the need for unification in what the school presented as its curricular offerings. Within this unification, he proposed what he described as the "CIA" approach to curriculum effectiveness:

> Correlation of subjects
> Integration of subjects
> Articulation of subjects

In terms of *correlation*, Dr. Allen noted that, traditionally, the curriculum for many teachers at the high school has connected with a number of outside influences. He asserted that these could include textbooks for individual classes, standardized tests such as ISTEP (Indiana Statewide Test for Educational Proficiency), state curriculum guides (of which, he noted, each teacher should have a copy), college and university requirements, standards of different interest groups such as NCREL (North Central Region Educational Laboratory), local standards and benchmarks, along with a number of other factors. Certain aspects of the correlations he listed were foreign to the teachers; when teachers were asked if they had ever contacted college or university personnel about curriculum components that would satisfy higher education pre-requisites, not one teacher indicated he or she had done so. Consequently, Dr. Allen asked if any of the teachers were *at all* familiar with the Indiana college entrance requirements (as discussed earlier, and published as part of the school handbook). Again, no teacher affirmed knowledge of these components. Dr. Allen envisioned the prospect of pursuing multiple sources of correlation as beneficial to the evaluation and improvement of the curriculum at Neosho and asked the teachers to familiarize themselves with the criteria necessary for university admission for their students.

The staff was also asked to consider how they *integrated* their subject matter into the entire school program. Dr. Allen suggested that this might take place both *between* and *within* vocational and academic areas; in other words, the industrial arts faculty may consider conducting a thematic unit with the language arts department, or the math department may develop some interdisciplinary work with the science teachers. To this end, it was noted, such multi-area learning was designed to allow students "windows" to see the practical nature of the subject matter and how solutions might be applied to real-life problems. However, the faculty once again acknowledged little progress in this area; and nearly all teachers (as will be shown further) individually asserted a lack of simple communication and interaction between departments in the building, much less taking the time to plan extensive, complex, thematic units.

Further highlighting the need for effective communication, Dr. Allen prompted discussion on the various ways that the teachers *articulated* their curricula. He proceeded to break down the term "articulation" into that which was *horizontal* and *vertical*. With the idea of horizontal articulation (or "scope" as it is commonly known), teachers were asked to consider how their subject matter was communicated across their individual levels – be it ninth grade History, tenth grade English, or other. In this instance, the staff envisioned the entire long-term plan of their courses; in other words, they were being asked to consider, "What am I accomplishing in my 180 school days?" On another plane (and one for which certain teachers would later express a greater concern) was the notion of vertical (or "sequential") articulation – "How effectively is the curriculum of the entire high school being transferred from grade to grade?" As noted earlier, a dearth of communication existed within the building. In some cases, this silence was even present *within* subject areas – including those with only two persons comprising the department. In individual interviews, many teachers viewed this as a concern. To many, however, an even larger dilemma was the vertical articulation that existed with the elementary school. Although resting on the same property as the high school (the two schools are, in fact, physically connected), the elementary school seemed to exist in a vacuum; little discourse ever appeared to take place between the two levels, either formally or informally. Several high school teachers presented this fact as a major curricular concern for them, particularly for those whose instruction included all of the K-12 grades (namely art, chorus, band, and physical education). When a student leaves one level, little information is forwarded to the next teacher as to what was accomplished. It was evident that many of the high school teachers spent the first three or four weeks of the school year simply evaluating what the students had previously learned. Furthermore, some teachers stated that the academic content changes from individual elementary teachers from year to year, making it difficult to even ascertain what one teacher's students will bring to the class each term. The idea of vertical alignment between the elementary and high schools was an attainable goal in the minds of many of the high school teachers, but the willingness to open the lines of communication appeared to be a serious impediment. Perhaps in an effort to allay this concern, Dr. Allen announced that the staff would be meeting with the elementary faculty in the following February or March to pursue more dialogue about what knowledge and skills they would like to see from students arriving at the high school. To this end, the high school teachers were asked to list the pre-requisite knowledge and skills for grade seven and nine entrants and have this information available for the subsequent meeting (the meeting planned for February or March, however, did not materialize). At this point Delila, the art teacher who served all grade levels in the school, noted that some systems have elementary schools in which the students maintain the same teacher and self-contained classroom for three straight years (such as in the second, third, and fourth grades – sometimes referred to as "looping"); it was considered that implementing such a program at Neosho would help alleviate the communication problem.

In the next stage of the meeting, Dr. Allen presented the idea of curriculum *development*; specifically, he asked the question, "What general instructional strategy are we going to follow?" When the question was raised, several eyebrows around the room were raised as well. Many staff members appeared nervous about being asked to follow a unilateral curricular or instructional strategy, one to which each and every staff member would be asked to comply. Sensing a bit of tension, Dr. Allen offered two more questions – questions basic to the study of curriculum: "What do you want students to know? Or, what do you want them to be able to do?" He attempted to further soften the tension by suggesting that pedagogical strategies should indeed be varied, including components such as personal visions, beliefs, goals, objectives, tasks, methods of evaluation, mission statements, and so forth. However, he asked the teachers to seek a certain degree of uniformity as to what was accomplished with the overall curriculum of the school. In particular, he cited the need for *alignment* within academic areas. In this regard, teachers were asked to consider the value of content consistency in their classes; staff members teaching different sections of the same course should pursue an acceptable degree of similarity in what was being taught, and how student learning was being evaluated.

As the meeting came to a close, the staff was given forms to complete. On the forms, each individual teacher was asked to list objectives that were currently covered in the courses he or she taught and the number of days that was spent on each objective. When this was requested, Rudy, a veteran teacher, raised his hand to speak. "I'm going to say something that probably nobody else here wants to say," he noted plainly. In an encouraging tone, Dr. Allen mentioned, "Well, I do want to hear whatever is on anyone's mind." Rudy continued, "I think this is a complete waste of time. I've seen these things come, and I've seen these things go. Nothing that we do now is going to change anything!"

This statement summarized the unspoken reluctance of several in the room; many teachers, particularly the older staff members, had been through curriculum revision efforts many times. During an interview session, another veteran teacher voiced this reluctance as well, yet with a certain degree of compassion for the administration.

> I understand why Dr. Allen brought it up, because it's probably his responsibility. That makes sense, but most of us who have been here forever, we've done it so many times that it's really old. We do it, and then we don't think about it again until someone else comes along, and then we have to do it again.

However, due to state pressure for accountability, occasional local pressure for performance, or other reasons, most staff members also saw the need for identifiable, common criteria for guiding the instructional efforts of the school. Hence, a storm of mixed emotions arose. Dr. Allen then posed the question, "Do we have standards right now?" Steve replied by simply saying "No." Dr. Allen then asked, "Do we have benchmarks?" Again, Steve responded for the group by asserting "No." As the meeting adjourned, the teachers were thereby asked to consider what standards and benchmarks would be important to them as representative of Neosho High School graduates and that this information would provide the basis for the next meeting.

Two peripheral factors appeared to contribute to the uncertain atmosphere of the meeting: the relative youthfulness of the staff, and consequently, their lack of experience in discussing curriculum. Over half (10 out of 19, or 53%) of the full-time staff had two or less years of teaching experience entering the 1997-98 school year, of which six (32%) were in their *first* year. Many of these younger teachers expressed an understandable discomfort with idea of curricular revision, simply due to this being their first professional experience.

As noted earlier, Powell (1991) recommended a three-step process for administrators to enlist teacher participation in curriculum revision in small schools: an initial organizational meeting, the formation of a 3-5 member teacher council on curriculum issue, and the consequent delegation of specific curricular duties to all staff members. In considering this recommendation in the context of Neosho, Dr. Allen utilized the initial step with the staff meeting, but decided to skip step two; rather, he wished that each department (as implied in step three) would immediately begin forming their own goals and objectives for a new curriculum.

Interestingly, however, no teachers (either during this meeting or in subsequent interview sessions) spoke of a particular desire to teach any new courses at the high school. Most appeared content with the teaching duties that they had, seeking only to do an acceptable job with the requirements which they had been hired to perform. Furthermore, almost every faculty member did understand the importance of a comprehensive and diversified curriculum to ensure the success of the students in the "outside world." As with most contemporary discussions of curriculum expansion, the issue surfaced of increased technological capabilities for the building. There is one computer teacher in the building, Dante, a man who is an English teacher by trade; his skills allowed him to conduct the computer applications for the building as well. Dante in particular recognized the importance of technology training for the students of Neosho amidst the ever-growing, increasingly-connected outside world.   He would like to see a larger financial and curricular investment in computers, but he is aware that resources will not allow that to happen in the near future.

The School Board and Curricular Decision Making

The Neosho school system is served by a five-member school board which, at the time of this study, was composed of individuals not elected by the general public, but rather "appointed" by village trustees. It was the overwhelming consensus of the high school staff that an electoral process was needed, as the qualifications of many long-standing individuals were questioned by several people. The process of "appointment" had led to, in essence, a lifetime contract for certain board members, and the teachers generally felt that this situation contributed to an unchanging, inflexible school system and curriculum. Furthermore, the impact that the board had on the process of curricular revision appeared to be minimal. As seen in cases examined previously (Manges & Wilcox, 1997; Queitzsch & Nelson, 1996; Moriarity, 1981), the board members appeared to leave most curricular decisions up to the principal, with little input from themselves. Nonetheless, it is relevant to discuss the characteristics of the board, as its operation contributed to the discord present on the teaching staff in discussing the curriculum.

The final board meeting of the 1997-98 academic year was held on May 21st. Since the school does not possess an adequate conference room, the school library was used for the gathering. The author arrived at the meeting expecting to be the only witness; on the contrary, he found nearly the entire teaching staff (of both the elementary and high school) present, as well as the county sheriff, local civic leaders, and other citizens. It was learned that the teachers were pressing the board for a contract for the following year, an issue which the board was reportedly ignoring for some time despite continuous staff requests. The teachers crowded into the library as the board went about its usual review of minutes, voting procedures, and the entertainment of new business.

As part of the new business to be discussed, the teachers began their anticipated verbal assault on the board. Both experienced and younger teachers spoke, displaying their frustration about salary and workload as well as the contract situation. As with most teachers, Delila expressed her concern with the low pay for the Neosho staff. However, she also noted that the low salary was even less tolerable when compounded by the multiple duties that surround teachers at the school. She also highlighted the high rate of teacher turnover that continued to plague the district.

> In a larger school, I would be teaching, at most, four classes. Here, I prepare for *nine*. We will continue to lose our best teachers to other schools at an increasing rate; it has already begun. This year we have six first-year teachers; right now, I know of five teachers who do not

plan to return next year at least. This creates a great strain on the rest of the faculty. They must pick up the slack of the new teachers, as well as teach and guide their students. As a single parent, I was unable to afford to purchase the family group insurance plan. The result was that my son was uninsured for four years. To make ends meet, I've always worked a summer job. This year, I also took a part-time job teaching at [Freeport].

When people ask me if I'll be teaching here next year, I reluctantly answer that unless I get another offer I cannot refuse from a nearby district, I will be here. I wish I could answer, "Yes, this is where I want to be."

Other teachers, such as Monica, were aware of the low pay and extra duties when they took their jobs at Neosho; in return, they only wanted the simple appreciation of the board, as she asserts.

When I came to [Neosho], I realized that my salary was not going to be comparable to that of a larger school, but I also knew that there could be a lot of advantages to a smaller school... I would just like a little appreciation. The inability to come to terms on our contract demonstrates a lack of appreciation. All I ask is for a contract that shows I'm valued.

Elementary teachers were also present at the meeting, and their concerns were summarized by one of the veteran staff members.

This is a staff that, several years ago, agreed to wait on their paychecks so that the school would not have to borrow money. We realize that some [people] in the community think that teachers make too much money already. But, should workers get paid less than others, simply because they live in [Neosho]? We certainly do not work less than other teachers, and we feel that we should be paid comparably. Frankly, by asking us to change the insurance benefit from a percent to a fixed dollar, you're [the school board] asking some of us [the teachers] to take a pay cut.

The board seemed to pay little attention to the teachers' pleas, and the regular business of the meeting continued. Much of the meeting consisted of the review of both the elementary and high school parent handbooks, in which Dr. Allen and the elementary principal were asked to explain proposed changes to the wording within the text. Many teachers in the audience sighed, gestured, and even laughed in frustration when certain board members belabored what they perceived as moot or trivial points. They continued with other business, including the rejection of Dr. Allen's proposal of asking student-athletes to pay for half of their letter jackets (to this point, the school had paid the full amount for all the jackets).

Upon leaving the meeting, one of the staff members noted his frustration to the author. "They [the board] won't approve a raise so that we can get and keep quality teachers," he observed, "But it's funny how they will still pay for the kids' letter jackets."

This echoes the words of Peshkin (1978), as long-standing board members are likely to continue the time-honored traditions of the community. Sher (1983) also noted that the most prominent stakeholders in curriculum discussions – the teachers, who execute the curriculum – are the ones often left out of the process by school boards. Negative feelings towards schools boards have long been present, as noted by Cubberly (1912). "As a body they are exceedingly conservative, and hard to educate; they usually possess important powers; and, because they control the purse-strings, they frequently assume an authority unwarranted by their knowledge of school work" (p. 7). On a positive note, several teachers at Neosho envisioned the recent re-organization as a step towards positioning more qualified board members, and a curriculum that would be approved by compassionate, educated adults.

No decisions were made about curriculum at this board meeting. In fact, one teacher who had attended every board meeting throughout the year said the issue of curriculum was *never* raised.

But there was hope for some, as a new system of organization would be implemented for the selection of school board representatives in the future. As of January 1, 1998, the public schools in the town of Neosho embarked on a "community" system, as opposed to the "consolidated" system that had governed it since complying with the Indiana School Reorganization Act of 1959, as recalled by one of the veteran teachers on the staff:

> I was born and raised here; it's always been "[Neosho]
> Consolidated Schools" for as long as I can remember,

which turned out to be a consolidation of the two townships
that presently make up the school district. That was done
about, I think 1949 or 1950 – a little bit before my time.
The change that we're about ready to experience simply
reflects the school district being in compliance with the
1959 School Re-Organization Act, which, from what I
understand, the state told us we must do if we ever want to
add onto the building, remodel, or whatever.

With a population that expects significant growth in the next
decade, the town saw this action as necessary to obtain permission
from the state to build upon the existing physical structure. More
importantly to some, however, was that the status of Neosho schools
as a community system would allow citizens to be elected to the
board rather than appointed. Furthermore, several teachers noted that
a community system would allow for more Neosho citizens to be on
the board, rather than those currently serving who were from the
outlying, consolidated townships.

Staff members at the high school appeared to have varying
levels of respect for the local school board. Generally, the
experienced teachers were more wary of the decisions the board
made, whereas the younger staff members did not seem to know
much about what transpired at board meetings – though feeling
pressured to "maintain the status quo" in terms of instructional
strategies. Most wished to see an elected board, while a few others
wanted to see the current system of "appointments" continued
(certain village trustees were automatically guaranteed places on the
school board). In any event, the matter of *how* the representatives
assumed their positions on the board was not the biggest issue for the
high school teachers. Rather, the education levels of the members –
and the decisions that were being made by these members
(particularly as they related to curriculum) – caused the most concern.
Specifically, some teachers even wondered about the literacy skills of
one of the board members, as noted with the following comment:

> It's common knowledge that one of the board members
> cannot read and write – it frightens me that decisions are
> being made about the curriculum by these types of people.

Also in a skeptical tone, another teacher stated:

> I know that it's [the "community school" title] related to
> how the board is chosen, as opposed to kind of being
> picked right now, it'll be elected. It could be a difference,
> or it may not. I don't know the guys on the board – I really
> don't. I know who they are, but I don't know a lot about
> their background. From what I've heard from other people
> in the community, some of them aren't really well-
> educated. I don't think it's good to have someone on the
> school board who is illiterate. I think it would be good to
> have someone with a background such as a college degree,
> someone who is well-educated, who can run a business –
> someone with more than just a high school diploma.

And another teacher expressed concern about the lack of
day-to-day knowledge that the board had about the operation of the
school:

> Now, there's a state law saying that we cannot have a town
> board be a school board also, or something like that – we
> have to appoint them somehow. We're going to lose state
> money that way. I think it's a good idea; in small
> communities like the one I came from, we've got too many
> people on the school board that really didn't know what
> was going on in the schools, and they didn't care. It was
> just a status position kind of thing, and that happens more
> in the smaller schools than the larger schools. They still
> have to be voted in by the community, but they have to
> have certain credentials before they're qualified to be voted
> in. If someone's sitting on a school board, and they've
> never been in a teacher's position before, it's kind of hard
> for them to understand what we're going through.

The age of the school board members was a concern for
other teachers. Some felt that an influx of younger members of the
community on the board would improve the schools, as noted by the
following comment:

> I was all for the re-organization, because I did not feel our
> school board was representing the community very well; I
> felt the older farmers of the community were a little more
> prominent, because the town trustees are basically on the
> school board; they were never elected. Now, I believe that

a school board should be elected; maybe people who are in
their thirties instead of their sixties.

Other teachers were not as sure about how the re-
organization would affect the characteristics or demographics of the
school board, much less its impact on curriculum. Delila expressed
her views on this topic.

> Well, basically, as I understand it [the re-organization], it's
> a different way of getting a school board. Basically, it will
> give local people more of a say of who we have on our
> school board. It changes the setting on the map; which
> sections have certain representation. So, that's generally
> what I understand of it. I don't think it will change, a
> whole lot, how the school is being run at this time.
> Basically it means, once we've reorganized, we can now do
> things that before, under law, we couldn't do.

As evidenced by these statements, the teachers had varying
degrees of respect and concern for the current school board members
and the impact that these representatives had on the curriculum.
Some were fearful that improper decisions were being made by
ignorant individuals, while others felt that the board did not directly
influence curricular decisions. Certainly, some decisions made by the
board did affect the entire staff, such as those dealing with contract
concerns, salary negotiations, and other areas. Despite the variance in
opinion about the current board members, most teachers looked
forward to the future, when Neosho would have an elected school
board, as opposed to the current system of appointment. The
disenchantment with the board was part of what was seen as an
unfavorable working environment for the teachers.

The school board appeared to have little impact in the area
of curricular revision. Teachers mostly felt free to implement new
content or strategies (although, as will be discussed further, many
younger teachers were hesitant to do so without guidance). It was the
impression of the author that the board would have little input if the
teachers decided to reform the curriculum; the board seemed to "wash
its hands" of the issue and allow the teachers and the principal to
construct any plan they wish. Inefficiency seemed to plague every
move that the board made, and some of the teachers felt that the
board was too large – even at just five members – to operate

effectively. To be sure, an over-abundance of school employees has in some cases bogged down the rural educational system – especially in the case of board members. This was also detected early in the 1900s by Cubberly (1912), pointing in particular to the state of Illinois where, at one point, there were actually *more than twice as many* school board representatives than teachers.

> In Illinois, for example, about forty thousand district trustees (called directors there) [and called board members today] and township officers are necessary, by the law, to carry on the rural and ungraded schools of the state, though only about twelve thousand teachers are employed, less than that number of schools are maintained, and the total cost for maintenance is only about three million dollars a year. (pp. 33-34)

But in the opinion of many at Hickory, *nothing* would have made the standing board more efficient.

Summary

The unstable employment situation at Neosho High School, in part, had led to an unstable curricular situation. Due to the high turnover rate of teachers *and* administrators, few felt confident in devoting much time or effort to producing a new curriculum. Many were fearful that the curricular direction would change with the arrival of the next principal – which, when figured mathematically in looking at the history of the school, would occur within three years. Although teachers understood the need to re-evaluate the curriculum in light of the growing community, the turbulent trend of ever-changing administrative regimes had worn their enthusiasm for this endeavor.

Nonetheless, the staff members at Neosho – notwithstanding their previous experiences, successes, and failures with curriculum development – had been asked by the current school administration to address the topic. Faculty experiences within this realm had indeed varied greatly; some teachers had ventured into this arena many times, while younger staff members were getting their first taste of the process. Enthusiasm for the idea seemed to reside within the junior faculty, perhaps as a means of better understanding their own subject area, as well as that of others. Most of the more experienced teachers, however, remained pessimistic about the benefits such an activity might produce, as similar attempts had been made in the past with, at best, uncertain results. Being indigenous to the community, a couple of these older educators found the curriculum status quo to be suitable for the current needs of the town and precluded the need for further discussions of the topic – at least at the present time. Interestingly, some noted that previous efforts at curricular reform did not benefit students in even the smallest regard and that this factor should be strongly entertained before another overhaul takes place.

When considering a topic as important as curriculum, a small, rural school system must not assume that it has the advantage of a close-knit teaching staff. Two or three individuals that comprise an academic department may have no idea what each other is doing in their classrooms. Care must be taken in providing forums for curricular discussion. As noted earlier, this discussion cannot be forced; however, *opportunities* for discussion must be present, as little initiative may otherwise be taken to do this important work.

This discord was compounded by a school board that appeared inflexible, if not disinterested, in curricular matters. As the teachers claimed that the board members had little formal educational experience, they felt hesitant in involving the board in curricular discussions. As will be seen shortly, this had a particular impact on the younger teachers who often felt great isolation in looking for a formal curriculum from which to begin their teaching.

10. Prospects for the Production of a New Curriculum at Neosho

> Failure is instructive. The person who really thinks learns quite as much from his failures as from his successes.
>
> – John Dewey

As shown by the background discussion, a significant variance of opinions, teaching styles, philosophies, prior experiences, and other factors contributed to an unstable curricular situation at Neosho High School. This fact may be surprising when one considers the size of the school and the tendency to see small, rural schools as more cohesive than larger, urban school systems. Neosho is among the smallest high schools in Indiana and consequently possesses one of the smallest full-time teaching staffs. Under such circumstances, one might imagine that there would be some semblance of unity among the staff, be it in simple communication if not a shared philosophy. Interestingly, however, little interaction appeared to be present among the staff, much less a sense of unity. While such a school might use its small size to its advantage (through an enhanced atmosphere of communication), the teachers at Neosho let this potential advantage fall by the wayside.

Difficulties in the Pursuit of a New Curriculum

The task of developing a new curriculum for Neosho High School was generally viewed as extremely daunting by the staff, despite the fact that the school is among the smallest in the state. On the surface, one might think that such a small size would encourage teachers to engage in curriculum discourse; the mere proximity of a few individuals could create an open environment. However, in looking at the responses given in interviews by the teachers, the review of the current documents, and general observations made by the author, three major themes emerged that showed a lack of progress in this area: the high turnover rate of staff members, the failure to make use of past efforts to reform the curriculum, and – most prominently – the patterns of dysfunctional communication that existed in the school system. The problems with communication were multi-faceted, including a lack of an introduction to the curriculum for new staff members (as a by-product of the high turnover rate), a lack of consistency in the skills and knowledge taught in the elementary school, and the absence of simple interaction *between* and *within* departments in the high school. These themes emerged as significant barriers to the administration's goal of reforming the curriculum.

The High Rate of Teacher Turnover

In terms of its *values* and *operation*, the town of Neosho appears to have changed little over the decades. "Ours is a conservative community," Steve observed, "and from what I gather, the community still wants the core curriculum [subject areas such as English, Mathematics, etc.] taught." In looking at most aspects of the town, one might believe that little *has* changed in Neosho in the past fifty years. Original buildings remain, and many of the same family names dominate the area as they did a century ago (Blanchard, 1884). "This community is against change," Steve continued. "If you doubt that, go look at the average year of the trophies in the trophy case. You can't dare take one of them out, because that was so-and-so's year, and so-and-so walks on water, even though he hasn't picked up a baseball bat or a basketball in 35 years; they're still living in the past."

However, when mixed with the fury of modern employment in American society, one witnesses substantial changes in employment dynamics at Neosho High School. Teachers and administrators alike typically hold brief tenures, which may have an impact on the curricular, instructional, and assessment practices that take place, as well as on the students themselves. The short stay by most staff members was due to a variety of factors, but was primarily due to two major realities: meager salaries at Neosho and the availability of jobs in other school districts.

As with many rural sectors across the United States, a low tax base has partially caused the remuneration for Neosho teachers to be at a sub-standard level (see Indiana Department of Education, 1998). Although alternatives have been considered by the Indiana General Assembly, the property tax system stands as the chief means of support for the state's public schools. As with other states, the per-pupil expenditure for individual school districts is in direct proportion to the value of local property. In 1998, Neosho schools spent $5,173 per student, while the Indiana average was $6,402 (Indiana Department of Education, 1998). Such figures contribute to the below-average teacher salaries at Neosho which, while attracting younger teachers who experience difficulty finding employment elsewhere, causes dissatisfaction after a few years. This pattern was noticed by Rudy, one of the veteran members of the faculty.

> We have tremendous turnover with teachers. We have a lot of kids [teachers] come here out of school, work one year, and they're gone, because they don't make much money. This is not a handy place to get to; they have to drive from [the large nearby city] or somewhere [further] away to get here.

Several of the teachers at Neosho were hired shortly before the start of the 1997-98 school year; furthermore, a few learned of their new jobs with less than a week's notice. During the author's interviews with these teachers, they revealed that this was their only job offer and that they accepted without giving much consideration to the community or the curriculum in place. Such behavior is generally witnessed in rural schools, as cited by Nachtigal (1992). "Many [new teachers] are in the rural school because they were unable to get a job in a larger urban or suburban community" (p. 76). Often, the philosophy of the new teachers may be in contrast to what is expected to be taught. In his influential writings on curriculum, Ralph Tyler

(1949) noted that the philosophy of a given community must underpin the answer to these questions. "It is necessary to screen the heterogeneous collection of objectives thus far obtained so as to eliminate the unimportant and contradictory ones. The educational and social philosophy to which the school is committed can serve as the first screen."

History has shown that ultimately at Neosho the low salary leads to much disenchantment, and a mass exodus of young, new teachers will follow. This trend is seen as detrimental not only to the curriculum, but to the very students as well – as noted by Jack, the second-year math teacher:

> We have 18 or 19 high school teachers, and you're talking three or four people [teachers leaving] a year every year, and that's a lot. And the kids – speaking of that, the kids last year (that was my first year), it's unbelievable how many kids came up to me and said, "Are you going to be here next year?" They just expect you not to come back, and I don't think that's very good. There's not a lot of consistency. I never asked [my] high school teachers if they were coming back; I just expected them to be there. And shoot, a lot of my teachers are still there! It just struck me as really funny how many kids asked that. They don't expect you to stick around. And I think that's sad – I think that's something that needs to be changed. I don't know how they'd change that, but it's something to work on.

It is obvious that Jack experienced stability with *his* high school teachers; the fact that almost all were returning the following year provided comfort for him, and a sense of caring for the student body. A majority of the teachers at Neosho did display care and compassion for their students, but teachers like Jack felt that a negative message was often sent by the staff members who left their jobs after a short time.

A few teachers, in particular those with young families, conveyed a greater concern for the salary range and for this reason questioned their ability to stay at Neosho for an extended period of time. Most of these staff members asserted their enjoyment of the school, the students, and the community, and expressed a desire to stay if the financial conditions were improved. Despite this fact, however, it is interesting to note that nearly all of the teachers (17 of

19) had chosen to live outside of the Neosho community even though their cost of living would have been significantly lower in Neosho – further indication of plans to leave their jobs in a short time. The average salary of a high school teacher at Neosho for the 1997-98 school year was $26,494, as compared with the state average of $38,345 (Indiana Department of Education, 1998).

As one of the elder teachers put it, "You can make more money by accident than what you get paid here."

This high turnover among the faculty causes great harm to the continuity of the curriculum, particularly as it relates to the many first-year teachers who are brought in each term. These individuals are asked to develop a curriculum of their own, as their predecessors leave them with nothing from which to start.

The Use of Past Curricular Reform Efforts
There was great frustration displayed by many teachers for the alleged misuse (or even "non-use") of prior curricular reform efforts, particularly with the Performance-Based Assessment (PBA) project undertaken in 1995. Despite the high turnover of faculty since the PBA assessment took place, there appeared to be a communal feeling of worthlessness about the project's results. This feeling existed among both faculty present at the time of its conception and those who were hired since and have heard of its impact (or lack thereof) on the school's curriculum. Those who were present for the PBA project described its construction as a painstaking process, requiring long hours after school and on weekends to have it come to fruition. Being under different administrative leadership at that point, many teachers, in retrospect, recalled feeling it would be "different this time"; that finally, the school system had found administrators who were there to stay and were genuinely interested in remaining to see their efforts ultimately benefit the school and community. Soon, however, "the process became a resume-builder for yet another person," as one veteran teacher put it. The principal at the helm of the project – the one who exhibited the most enthusiasm and promise for its benefits – soon after left to take a similar but more lucrative job in another school system in Indiana.

Several teachers felt nothing less than abandoned by this event and, understandably, became disheartened about pursuing any further curricular reform. In fact, when the current principal and superintendent arrived, staff members acknowledged that there was even a certain degree of "fear" that they would be asked to overhaul the content of their courses once again. The attitude of the school appeared in direct contrast to the five traits discussed earlier by Wall, et al. (1991) in building a positive future for the curriculum of such a school.

This attitude was an ominous prelude to the November staff meeting. The lack of a bona fide direction for the curriculum was made clear by Dr. Allen at the meeting. For some teachers, the inevitable request had finally arrived. It may be the case that Dr. Allen inherited an unfinished job with the school's curriculum. The preceding administrative team left no scope and sequence to follow, and thus the new principal began his curricular pursuits with two strikes against him: no cohesion to the curriculum as bequeathed by his predecessors, and consequently, a general apathy, dislike, or even hatred of curriculum development among his faculty. Starting in this unfavorable position, Dr. Allen assumed a monumental task in prompting the teachers to reconsider their curricula – not only in regard to what they taught in their own classrooms, but also in how the various departments and grade levels could work cooperatively and thematically.

Certain veteran teachers had experienced other curriculum development projects in the past – either at Neosho or previous places of employment – and seriously questioned the *focus* of most of these efforts. Teachers in this group (as well as some others) felt that the limited time they had would be better spent in addressing student needs. One teacher pointed out that, in the end, the work conducted on PBA resulted in no practical benefit for the students, and the staff needed to be assured of some such benefit being possible before a similar project was undertaken again, as one teacher expressed.

> One of the things I think the staff needs to know is that many of them are willing to do whatever it takes for one, a good performance evaluation, if that's what drives you; two, to be a "good little soldier," if that's what drives you; or three, most importantly, to benefit students. We need to be told, though, how PBA will benefit students. There was

not one single thing in PBA that benefited students. The staff needs to know why we did PBA when it didn't benefit the kids. If some of those teachers who are still pulling out the same lessons, same worksheets, same exams as last year would spend an hour looking at PBA and re-vamp their worksheets, the students would find tremendous relief in that – and that would be time well spent, because it would be aiding the kid. The staff needs to see how this will either make them better teachers, or that it will positively impact kids. Without that, any project – be it curriculum, athletics – is doomed. And we don't do a very good job of identifying why we're going to do things.

The same individual, however, also envisioned some benefit in re-evaluating the documents produced in the PBA discussions, perhaps serving as a catalyst for future possibilities with the curriculum.

Two years ago, we worked on PBA. I have to believe the people have invested themselves in that document. New teachers need to become familiar with the document, and there had to be enough seeds in that document that we could pull out parts of that as a basis for some of the things that the curriculum would do. Why do we want a curriculum, Dr. [Allen]? Well this, this, this, this. Some of those items that he's identified that he needs a curriculum for are contained or can be grown from the seeds that are already in the PBA, which people have invested time in, which people are proud of, and which has sat on a shelf now for two years... I think we have a core of people that have been here for so long, and have seen so many administrators, so many "grand plans," be it PBA or curriculum or Indiana 2000, everywhere from the governor's office on down to the PTA, they've seen so many of these come and go that they say, "Hey, I'm putting in time; I'm not going to invest myself, my time, my skills in another one of these aberrations that's going to sit on a shelf."

Many staff members, such as the individual above, were hesitant to devote any significant energy to additional curricular reform, since there was little historical evidence that their toils would produce a working document – or simply something that would benefit students.

The typical size of the departments at Neosho also influenced the ways that previous curriculum was used. As with many small-town high schools, certain departments within Neosho High School (particularly in elective areas) were comprised of only one or two faculty members. This characteristic provided interesting perspectives on producing new curricula or reorganizing curricula that were currently in use. Departments at the high school that consisted of one faculty member included agricultural education, industrial education, chorus and band, home economics, and foreign languages. Due to low student enrollment, individual faculty members also conducted other courses, such as Physics and Calculus. In many cases, teachers who singularly comprised the department envisioned the circumstances as an opportunity for tremendous curricular freedom; they felt great liberty in adjusting the curriculum to their needs and wishes, as well as to those of their students. This feeling was more common among experienced faculty members, who demonstrated confidence in their teaching methods and rapport with the administration and community. The home economics teacher noted:

> I *am* the home economics department. I have felt pressure to change [the curriculum] only because home economics has changed – from cooking and sewing to more family things. I mean, I don't even teach the classes that I was trained to teach when I started. We do family relations and interpersonal relations, consumer education – these things were not in existence twenty-five years ago. We had cooking and sewing; that was it. Even the methods of cooking have changed. So, we never have the same curriculum. The state is getting ready to make another change. It's not like history, where everything is the same and you just add-to.

In a similar tone, Rudy spoke of his considerable latitude in industrial education.

> When I came here, they had no program. There were eleven of us in the department at [Caledonia]; it was one of the largest in the state. I *am* the department here.

On the other hand, the younger teachers who were the lone members of their departments felt more trepidation about issues of curriculum. These fears ranged from being able to start their first year of teaching with an identifiable curricular document to the fearful prospect of producing *new* curricula for their areas. As could be expected, these teachers primarily sought to "get through the day" (or week, or even the entire year). And admittedly, these teachers gave little thought to matters of curriculum, and most were disappointed that an actual curriculum was not left behind by their predecessors. Several relied upon content recently learned in their college programs or occasional lesson ideas suggested by other staff members. These teachers also accepted their jobs with the added obligation of holding various extra-curricular duties which further reduced the time available to consider what was taught in their classrooms. Teachers in this group imagined great benefit when considering the production of a bona fide curricular document for the school – not so much for their own use, but for the well-being of future newcomers so as to help allay the fears of facing daily classroom instruction for the first time.

Communication with New Staff Members

The absence of communication existed in the form of a three-headed enemy against the curricular reform efforts at Neosho. The lack of dialogue was present in the integration of new faculty, dealings with the elementary school, and even between and within departments at the high school. This cluster of difficulties plagued efforts to ignite discussion on curriculum issues, which particularly affected the large contingent of new teachers.

As mentioned previously, over half of the full-time teachers (10 out of 19) were in either their first or second year in the profession. This situation appeared to contribute greatly to the lack of curricular discussion occurring among the staff; not only because of the relative inexperience of the faculty, but also due to the fact that, as stated earlier, many of these beginning teachers were left with little or no materials by their predecessors with which they might begin. Some of these new teachers were hired within a week before the start of school in August, thus compounding the difficulty they encountered in ascertaining the curriculum to be taught – much less considering its revision. Kathy, one of the first-year teachers, explained her frustration.

> *Nothing* – when I got here there was *nothing* [for a curriculum]. There were some keys in my desk, and I couldn't find anything they went to. That was it – that's all I had. I built what I teach from the ground up... I only got hired about two or three days before school started, so I didn't even have time to look over the books.

Kathy asserted that, in being fresh out of college, she was very anxious to find a job. Therefore, when the job at Neosho became available, she accepted it quickly. She wondered why the school board waited so long to fill the position but was nonetheless happy to be employed. She also directly experienced the subsequent problems of the departing teachers' failure to leave materials and suggestions for the curriculum. In terms of previous learning, she found herself, by default, relying on what her students told her.

> I've talked to the students about what they've studied. Since the teachers in the science department are all gone, there weren't any science teachers to ask. The kids are supposed to have chemistry in the 8th grade. So, I ask the kids what they covered in the 8th grade, and they said they did two chapters the whole year. They never got anything done. I get more input from the students, since they've had the teachers. That makes sense, because other teachers don't know what goes on in the other classrooms.

Isaiah, an English teacher, expressed a similar uncertainty about his first day in the classroom at Neosho. "I was never told anything about it [how the language arts curriculum was formed]," he said. "I just went to my class, and taught what I was told to teach." Renee, in the physical education department, likewise had a confusing start to her job. "I didn't even know what I was going to teach; I didn't have any idea," she admitted plainly. "The person before me was not here, the principal was gone, the superintendent was gone, and even our guidance counselor wasn't sure where the books were or if there was [*sic*] books." Mickey, another first-year teacher, added his perspective when asked about the presence of a curriculum for use on his first day. "Not that I know of; I developed one myself, basically." Finally Jack, who was in his second year of teaching math, echoed the same feeling. "When I came here, I wasn't told what to teach, how to teach. They [the previous administration] just said, 'Here's your class; here are your books; whatever you want to do, you can do.' The curriculum was whatever I wanted it to be."

Mickey continued to reflect on the fact that there was no curriculum upon his arrival.

> [For] my two 7th grade classes and my Earth Science class, I basically follow the book with those. The main reason for that is that I wanted to get my feet wet, and it doesn't hurt them to go by the book sometimes. But with the Bio I and Bio II classes, I developed my own curriculum for both of those... and I will leave it for whoever comes next year – because nobody did that for me.

Other beginning teachers conveyed similar feelings of abandonment, isolation, and helplessness in confronting the organization of content for their subject areas. Their teaching often took a "hand-to-mouth" format, with little opportunity for long-term unit or semester planning. Thus, in some academic areas, the departure of faculty members after only one or two years on the job caused two concerns: their replacement with qualified individuals on short notice, as well as the failure to leave behind curricular ideas. To this end, the school struggled in transferring its curriculum to its new faculty. As Small (1977) pointed out, the selection of a textbook often becomes *the* curriculum for the new teacher. As a result of poor transfer of materials and strategies from one teacher to the next, the various textbooks served as the curricula in many classrooms at Neosho.

Such frustrations for these young teachers were multiplied when an elective subject area entered the picture. Dave, who coordinated all of the band and chorus classes for the high school, mentioned that a lack of curricular organization by the previous music teacher had left him in a particularly difficult situation.

> I had to develop it [the music curriculum] myself, and I spent the first month playing some songs, just trying to find out where they were at. When I came in, there was no curriculum of what they had done. The bad thing is that the junior high and high school are together for the band, and

there are things that I have to cover for the junior high that
will bore the high school kids, and things that are too
challenging for the junior high kids that high schoolers
really need. So I've had to create my own curriculum, and
stay away from the books as much as I can... since I'm the
only one in the music department, I can pretty much do
what I want – nobody's telling me that I'm doing anything
wrong. The scary thing about that is, being a first-year
teacher, I had nothing to go by curriculum-wise, I would
just "try this, and see if it works."

It might be inferred that Dave has already participated in
"curriculum development" by saying that he has "had to create my
own curriculum." However, it is evident that this involved little long-
term planning (through no fault of his own). Not only was Dave left
with nothing by the previous band instructor, but he was also dealing
with a wide range of ages (grades 7 through 12) and talents (from
beginners to accomplished players), spending much energy and time
in diagnosing the abilities of his students. Dave mentioned that, in
the future, he would be interested in assisting the school with
curriculum revision; however, for the time being, he would like to
allow a complete trial run of "his" curriculum first. "As far as the
general curriculum of the school goes, I'm kind of waiting until the
end of the year (since it's my first year) to sit down and look at
everything," he said.

Even a few of the veteran teachers recalled a lack of
communication with their predecessors and the curriculum with
which they began. "If there was anything here before I came," an
experienced teacher said of her department's formal curriculum, "I
never saw it." Rudy also spoke of curricular absence in his area.
"When I came here, they had no program," he remembered. "This is
the information [displayed to the author] that I wrote up to establish a
program for Neosho High School." Finally Delila, who has taught art
for nine years, recalled the same feeling. "Nobody said to me, 'This
is what you're supposed to teach; here is what you're supposed to
cover.' They just said, 'Here is your classroom.'" The professional
courtesy of leaving a basic starting point for a replacement teacher,
therefore, has hardly been present at Neosho and is no small part of
the overall communication problem for the faculty.

Communication with the Elementary School Staff

As noted, Neosho Elementary School is located on the same property as the high school, and the two buildings are physically joined. A short hallway connects the two, but the hallway appears to be generally unoccupied during the school day. Little interaction seemed to exist between the two levels. While it is understandable that limited time is available during the day for the two staffs to communicate, the lack of dialogue extended to after-school hours as well. Before the arrival of Dr. Allen as the high school principal, few efforts had been made to set up meetings with the elementary faculty. Prior to making his decision to leave the school at the end of the 1998 school year, he had made this a priority for the future; but once again, he appeared to have been left little help by his predecessors in this regard (and ironically, he would now become a "predecessor" himself). Both schools have hardly any knowledge of the other's curriculum, and a "guessing game" ensued on the part of the high school faculty when a student arrived for his or her secondary education. The "guessing" involves the high school teacher attempting to ascertain the ability level of each individual student as it is evident that little information is passed along from the lower grades. This dilemma is compounded by elementary teachers who, according to the high school staff, do things differently with each passing year, making it difficult to determine the instruction students received in a particular teacher's class. This factor directly affected the curricular status of the math department at the high school, as those teachers pondered the challenges of the coming year.

The high school math teachers at Neosho (consisting of two individuals) were concerned with the prospects for course offerings for the 1998-99 school year. It was the feeling of one of the teachers that the lowest-level math course offered, General Mathematics and Problem Solving, had become a "dumping ground" for students incapable of succeeding in other courses (such as the next higher-level course, Pre-Algebra). Both the math department and high school administration had considered removing the course from the curriculum. This had been presented as a way to not only increase standards for the students but also to make better use of teachers' time. (In the spring of 1998, there were only six students enrolled in the General Math course.) Students at Neosho High School were required to pass two years of math for graduation and were encouraged by the counseling staff to begin their math coursework during the ninth grade year. This strategy was promoted as opposed to, for instance, attempting to satisfy the two-year requirement in the eleventh and twelfth grades just prior to graduation.

One of the math teachers cited the need for better preparation in the elementary grades in basic mathematic principles. If this occurred, the teacher noted, almost all students would be ready to begin pre-algebra when reaching the ninth grade. However, it was the consensus of both math teachers that many students are mathematically unprepared when they leave the elementary school and have little chance to complete the two-year requirement for graduation at the high school level. This has led to the faculty and administration considering the retention of the General Math course – at least until math instruction is enhanced at the elementary level and identifiable skills and knowledge are documented in this instruction as students enter the high school.

Other high school teachers expressed frustration with the elementary staff as well. Rudy, in the industrial arts department, also utilized math in his courses. However, he found himself re-teaching things that he felt should have been accomplished earlier. "We use math in here everyday," he stated plainly. "But I have to start every year at the beginning with teaching fractions – I mean, just start all over, like it was fourth or fifth grade, and teach the kids how to read the ruler, things like that." He went on to add, "I know a lot of kids that graduated from here who couldn't get out of the sixth grade if they had to pass a test." The idea of an "exit exam" for students before graduation from the high school was supported by some teachers (including Rudy), but dismissed by most. The majority of the staff felt that enough exams already existed and that such a test could not possibly match a new curriculum that would be produced.

Despite understanding the importance of improved communication, some of the high school teachers believed that better contact with the elementary school was simply not possible. Rooted in this feeling were factors such as time available to meet, the logistical differences between self-contained (elementary) and subject area (high school) classes, and the blunt lack of interest on the part of both sides. In a somewhat hopeless tone, Rudy determined that permanent "damage" had been done to students at the elementary level.

> I don't see how we can directly link what we do with the
> elementary. I think that what the elementary does is four or
> five times more important than what we do. I think
> basically, by the time a kid is out of the 6th grade, they can
> develop skills, but if they can't read and do math – and
> they've got to know it by then, or they'll never know it.
> And, I don't know how what we do, in any way, affects
> what the elementary does. They're done with when we get
> them – for good or bad.

A unique perspective on the issue of communication with
the elementary school was held by the teachers who serve all of the
K-12 grades. These included areas such as art, music, and physical
education. They witnessed, first-hand, the isolation of the two
schools, and the corresponding curricular difficulties. One of the
physical education teachers noted that the sequence of her curriculum
was easy to follow as students progress through the grades, but
understood that this sequencing may not be so apparent to teachers in
other departments.

> With me being both elementary and high school, it's easy
> to see how my curriculum flows from one level to the next.
> I really don't have trouble with that. I think it's good to get
> some kind of organization; there's not a whole lot of inter-
> activity with the elementary and high school teachers, even
> though I haven't been here that long. I think since the
> school is this size, it would be good.

In general, the high school teachers felt that an open line of
communication with the elementary school would be good for the
curriculum, but difficult to attain. In the meantime, they faced the
frustration of what they felt to be inadequately prepared students and
inconsistency of instruction from teachers at the previous level.

Communication Between and Within Departments at the High School
The most prominent difficulty in pursuing curricular
production was the lack of communication within the high school
itself – both inside individual departments, and among different
departments in an effort to construct some semblance of unit planning
across subject areas. Once again, the small size of Neosho High
School factored into this challenge. No more than three teachers

comprised any department at Neosho, with several containing only one. Thus, the entire concept of "communication" took on a unique role at Neosho, as with many small high schools. Because of small numbers, the *amount* of curricular discussion that takes place on curriculum within departments (and the *number of ideas* generated at such meetings) would naturally be minimal. Conversely, one might expect that this communication would also be clear, direct, conversational, and fruitful – also due to small numbers. Unfortunately, several departments at Neosho seemed to have minimal, unproductive conversation. In the departments in which one person comprises the faculty, that often individual maintains unilateral control of the organization, direction, and even the construction of the curriculum for the subject area with input from the administration.

While it is expected that high school teaching styles will vary from person to person, it may be equally expected that a certain amount of communication about course content should take place within academic departments in pursuit of alignment. Two of the major departments at Neosho, language arts and mathematics, had three and two teachers respectively. While the math teachers appeared to speak frequently with each other, the language arts faculty were not only different in their teaching styles, but tended to maintain a kind of personal isolation. Dante affirmed the lack of dialogue that exists and how this attitude affects the experiences of the teachers for the following school year.

> I would say that the biggest problem we face is a lack of cohesiveness within the department... kids will come into the classroom and say, "Well, we didn't cover that last year." It would be nice to say, "Oh yes, you did!" Honestly, sometimes you have to question, because you know that this person [another English teacher] does not like doing this [certain aspects of English instruction], so it's very possible that they skipped the entire unit on grammar or writing a research paper. It can happen.

In terms of personality, the three members of the language arts faculty were quite different. Dante was a young man, who had an interest in computers and technology and was in his third year of teaching. Isaiah was also a young staff member (in his second year), but his other interests were in sports and coaching, and he incorporated that realm into his teaching. Finally there was Wilma, a veteran teacher of 17 years at Neosho. Each of the three displayed a unique instructional style. Little was actually known about the day-to-day operations within each person's room, as highlighted by Dante. Isaiah noted that he and Dante made at least one effort to align the language arts curriculum for the school. "[We] talked a lot about what we taught last year, because we each had a group of eighth graders," he said. "So we would try to keep it relatively the same. We would switch classes, so they could hear another voice, and that was about as close as we got to curriculum development." Although it may not have contributed much to developing a curriculum, switching their classes allowed for some professional communication between them and presented students a broader range of instructional strategies. Wilma had no comment on the alignment of the language arts curriculum at the school but suggested that there was minimal discussion among the teachers.

One department at the high school demonstrated exceptional communication between its staff members. The social studies division, consisting of two individuals, displayed excellent alignment of its courses – despite the quite distinct content interests and teaching styles of the two persons. In personality and professional experience, the two were quite different. George was a veteran of 23 years in the Neosho school system and an indigenous resident of the community. Steve, on the other hand, worked in journalism for a short time before entering the profession of education four years ago. They admittedly pursued different aspects of historical and civic education because of personal interest and skill, but nonetheless they engaged in dialogue frequently about how these preferences could be harnessed into a quality program for their students. This was particularly noticed by Steve who had relied on George's input for the structure of his classes.

> How good is it? [the communication between George and him] I think on issues where it matters, we're both professional enough to realize that we better go get help from the other one. He's been doing this for a long time; he doesn't need to hear what a fifth-year teacher has to say. But he's always done that, and that's to his credit. We disagree on an awful lot, and our styles are vastly different,

and I'm sure that one thinks the other is doing it wrong at times. Bottom line is, we work well together when we have to.

As Steve suggested, the "disagreement" that was present at times between them was a positive reality; in the few other departments at the school that actually *did* communicate, the discussions appeared to be "yes" sessions for each other. Any idea offered was viewed as acceptable, and little constructive criticism occurred, apparently for fear of hurt feelings. A different professional understanding existed between George and Steve. If one questioned what the other was doing, the matter was not taken personally; rather, the recipient of the criticism understood that it was an effort to make him a better teacher, and thus further dialogue was generated. George maintained that he would like to do more for the social studies curriculum, but necessary time and resources were not available.

> I have longed for some civics instruction at the lower levels
> of high school – I would love to see it. I do not think that a
> semester of government is good enough. It just does not
> make the students prepared, and heaven knows we need to
> prepare citizens. I don't think we're doing enough. Maybe
> I'll see it, but right now Steve and I are tied up in about as
> much as we can be.

As exemplified by the social studies department, open lines of communication can alleviate the difficulties caused by personal interests or different teaching styles. The fact that these two teachers consistently conferred helped produce a smoothly-flowing program for the students, and a resulting wide breadth of material for a curriculum-in-use. This was accomplished, quite simply, because of the two teachers' willingness to create time to discuss curricular issues – issues that could also affect the learning experiences of their students in other classes.

It is likely that many teachers were unaware that their curricular choices greatly affected the fluidity and efficacy of instruction in other departments. For example, as Rudy noted this earlier, his industrial arts students lacked math skills necessary for his work – skills that he believed would be present by the time a student reached high school. One of the science teachers was also perplexed about this problem. "You have to have algebra before you can take chemistry," this person stated, "but I have at least five students who have never had algebra." Cindy, who teaches Spanish, wished to see communication opened up between departments so that teachers were not "re-teaching" things unnecessarily.

> I would like to see scope and sequencing, particularly with English and History. That affects my area, because sometimes I have to stop and teach geography, sometimes I'm teaching grammar – a kid doesn't know what a direct object or pronoun is in English, so he has no clue what it is in Spanish. I feel like I'm teaching or re-teaching from scratch from other areas all the time. I'll ask the kids, "Have you had any experience with Latin American history?" I'll try to find out what they know before I teach Spanish.

Once again, simple dialogue may help alleviate some of these problems. Available time for planning, grading, and other duties is often cited as a concern for teachers, but much time appeared to be wasted by staff members at Neosho due to isolation – both in a physical and a curricular sense.

Mistaken assumptions about curricula in other classes was another type of problem in this area. Some teachers either assumed that certain content was taught in particular classes or were judgmental about certain classes due to their titles. Susan, the agricultural educator, claimed that the stereotypes associated with her courses led others to believe that nothing from the core curriculum entered her teaching.

> I'm sure the other teachers have definite assumptions about what I'm teaching. In the general science class that has one student, I taught all that in my natural resources class – everything they covered, I taught in the same room... that's something that I'm going to have to go up against – the rest of the teachers saying, "Well, that can't be science credit." Then I'll have to get my curriculum out and say, "Oh yes it is!" So, from that aspect, I'd like the other teachers to know what I'm doing, and I'd like to know what they're doing. We have small classes here, and I think a lot of the teachers could team-teach.

It was evident that much content was taught repeatedly in multiple classrooms at Neosho and caused a waste of teachers' and students' time. Dante, in the English department, believed that a certain policy also contributed to "content overkill." He pointed out that if a student fails a class, he/she is allowed to repeat it time and time again; there was no limit to the number of re-takes for a course. With this policy in place, "They [the students] just know they can take it [the course] over again," he claimed.

Interestingly, the majority of the teachers at Neosho *were aware* that a communication problem existed among the departments – even the first-year teachers. Dave, the rookie music instructor, noticed this immediately. "As far as the curriculum goes, it's been my experience that everyone around here is on their own; the math department is the math department, and they don't correspond with the English department." Despite knowledge of this deficiency, however, little was suggested for how to remedy it. Nearly the entire faculty envisioned a better working environment and manageable curriculum through improved dialogue, but few seemed willing to initiate the process. The enacted curriculum (as defined earlier) that each teacher brought to the classroom remained insulated within his or her walls; and, since communication was poor between and within departments, it was halted at the doors of individuals teachers as well. Steve was particularly troubled by this idea, in considering that his freedom for teaching to his desires was counteracted by an apathetic attitude of his peers.

> There's no oversight [to the curriculum]. No one knows what I do down here, outside of myself and my students. Parents, for the most part, are uninformed, the administration, for the most part, is uninformed... our curriculum is what I say it is. I would gladly march to whatever drumbeat was out there; unfortunately, I'm the only one with sticks and a drum, so I'm picking my own beat.

Understandably, this concept of "picking my own beat" was troublesome to some of the new teachers. One of the first-year teachers said plainly, "Because there was no curriculum, I was completely lost on my first day of teaching, and I got scared in a hurry." Another new teacher picked up on the "game" quickly.

"Honestly, I could make my lesson plans look like I am teaching everything that I am supposed to be; I can just fill in those little boxes," this person offered. "But, the principal cannot be in the room everyday, and unless a close-circuit TV monitor is put in, well... ." It is evident that few teachers at Neosho had taken the time to consider what is being taught in other classes, and the result was a dysfunctional curriculum in which subject matter was repeated unnecessarily, younger teachers felt "lost," and opportunities grew scarce for relating subjects across an interdisciplinary theme. Certain teachers, such as Jack, expressed an interest in a thematic curricular component. He believed it would be a good idea, at the very least, to investigate. "There is no cross-subject area participation here," he figured. "And I don't know if that would be good or not; maybe at the junior high to do that, but certainly in the high school, there's not a lot of that."

Steve put the curricular communication problem in another way. In his previous work with a radio station, he once asked the news director what "news" actually was. "He looked at me and said, 'News is what I say it is.' I think to some extent, and I think it's unfortunate, our curriculum is what I say it is."

11. Summary of the Curricular Status at Neosho

A secret is something that you tell one person at a time.

– A wise man from Neosho

As with many educators across the nation, the faculty at Neosho High School had witnessed the arrival and departure of many curricular reform activities over the years. Some of these arrivals were more warmly embraced than others, and some were more productive or efficient than others. In retrospect, however, almost every scenario was viewed by veteran staff members as "resume-builders" for the administrators in place, administrators who would not call Neosho home for very long thereafter. With such school leaders seeming to use the Neosho system as a "stepping stone" to more favorable opportunities, several teachers became defensive about deconstructing the curriculum time and time again. This segment of the staff was counteracted by a younger contingent, who, for the most part, were eager to engage in the curriculum development process but had few materials or experience from which to begin. This contingent remained a significant force year after year, as many teachers at Neosho were leaving their jobs annually, and new people were being integrated on a yearly basis.

In addition to these difficulties, the staff was mired in a larger communicative problem. Without discourse transpiring about issues of curriculum, most departments were left to fend for themselves, and teach to whichever strengths or interests suited their members. This resulted in the repetition of much academic content across different departments. Although it may be argued that some skills and content are worth teaching a second or third time through, any such occurrences did not happen by plan at Neosho; they happened by accident. Furthermore, they often happened with content that teachers believed should have been mastered in the earlier grades, such as work with fractions in mathematics that had to be performed in the vocational classes in the high school.

Thus, as the teachers themselves admitted, faculty prospects for the production of a new curriculum at Neosho High School were extremely poor. Teachers were generally aware of the problems, such as inadequate communication, use of prior reform efforts, and high staff turnover. However, few teachers knew of practical solutions to these difficulties, and fewer yet seemed willing to pursue *new* solutions. The curriculum status quo at Neosho was indeed working for many teachers. Several enjoyed the freedom afforded by the little interaction that existed with their own department members, and other departments as well. For the most part, however, the inexperienced staff members – comprising the majority of the staff, in fact – felt lost due to this isolation. It was these first- and second-year teachers themselves who saw the most benefit in a formal, written curricular document, so that future newcomers would not experience the helpless feeling of not knowing what to teach.

The majority of the teaching staff at Neosho High School displayed genuine concern for their students. Many teachers at the school appeared to work very hard at their jobs and took great pride and joy in witnessing the successes of their labors. Several teachers undertook multiple extracurricular assignments (at no extra pay) to help provide a variety of activities for students. The school was led by a supportive, empathetic principal, who worked tirelessly to provide a positive environment for teachers and students. Unlike the alleged selfishness of previous administrators, Dr. Allen demonstrated a commitment to the long-term efficiency of the school, as exemplified by his proposed overhaul of the curriculum.

The small population and compact physical size of Neosho should have facilitated a productive arena for curricular discourse among the faculty; unfortunately, it did not. Communication – in all fairness, a concept that people in many professions take for granted – was noticeably absent and was both the cause and effect of numerous difficulties associated with revising the curriculum. Much of this dilemma was not the fault of the staff employed at the time; several predecessors of the 1997-98 staff had apparently left their jobs in an unprofessional, unhelpful manner, leaving no assistance for the individuals who were to take their places. But the question may be asked: is this assistance morally obligated, or otherwise necessary? Or rather, should teachers (even ones in their first year) be left to develop their own curricula and thus leave their own imprint on the culture of the school? It is the perspective of the author that teachers should expect *some* degree of professional courtesy from those who came before them; the act of leaving behind ideas that did *not* work would even be of some benefit, so that the new teacher would not waste time with measures that were previously unproductive.

The recommendations below may not serve as infallible solutions for school districts that are similar to Neosho. As noted in the review of the literature, the history of educational policy in the United States has often pointed to a "force-fitting" of unilateral doctrines on all rural schools. Ideas constructed by educators and legislators at the national and state levels were often seen as applicable to every agrarian system, whereas many local districts interpreted the policies in various ways. Consequently, some of the difficulties witnessed at Neosho may not be present in school systems of a similar size and location, and yet other problems may exist. However, the themes that emerged from this study may, at the very least, be caveats for similar school systems that are considering curriculum development.

It would be a mistake to assume that the agrarian nature of the Neosho community diminishes the academic aspirations of its students. Although many young people displayed an interest in pursuing farming as a career (as discovered through casual conversation with students and the comments made by teachers), many others dreamed of a college education. This diversity of desire commands a comprehensive and diverse curriculum, one that meets the rigors of university entrance requirements and examinations, as well as the foundations for agrarian occupations. Efforts need to be made – not only at Neosho, but in all American schools – to make sure that such dreams may be realized, and that issues such as dwindling property tax support do not impede this pursuit. Whether through distance learning technologies, joint instructional efforts on the part of multiple schools, or a wide-scale overhaul of state school funding systems, the students in rural sectors of the United States need to be assured that their academic needs and interests will be accommodated. Much of the onus of this responsibility is on the teachers who choose to work in rural settings.

It is a foregone conclusion that good teachers are necessary for a good school. Due primarily to multiple responsibilities and low salaries, Neosho is a stark example of a rural school system that cannot retain many quality teachers. As witnessed by the data discussed earlier in this study, several teachers leave their jobs at Neosho each year. The continuity of the curriculum and instructional practices are negatively altered by this trend, and the result is a downward cycle that appears difficult to reverse.

Recommendations

In an effort to enhance the process of curricular dialogue and revision among the staff at Neosho High School, the following recommendations are suggested by the author:

Increased alignment within subject areas. The nature of the small staff at Neosho High School (even in the most traditional academic divisions) should serve as an asset to discussion and decision-making processes within and between the various departments. Consequently, communication should not only be open, but also frequent; ideas on curriculum and course reform can be as casual as a conversation or as formal as regularly-scheduled meetings. This desirable atmosphere, however, did not seem to exist in certain departments of the high school. In some cases in which two or three people constituted the department, one teacher knew little or nothing about the topics or exercises being conducted in the other's classroom. Better communication, coupled with a willingness to incorporate new ideas into one's teaching, could foster a more positive outlook as to the comprehensiveness, flexibility, and overall quality of the curriculum, both within individual departments and the school as a whole. For this to occur, however, the faculty must be willing to embrace such discourse and make consistent effort to keep a periodic schedule of meetings. In order to promote this type of environment, informal discussions and gatherings during out-of-school hours should be considered as alternatives to finding time during the congested school day.

Increased / improved communication with the elementary school. As a general rule, almost all of the teachers in the high school note spending three to four weeks at the beginning of the school year in basic diagnostics. It is the consensus of the teachers that the instruction students have received from the elementary school is varied and uncertain, that no assumptions about previous learning can be made, and that a great amount of pre-testing (and informal evaluation as well) is necessary at the start of the academic term. In a community and school system as small as Neosho, it is imperative that consistent, regular dialogue takes place between the elementary and high schools. Too much is at stake – namely, an exorbitant amount of teacher time for diagnostics, continuity of the overall curriculum, and general instructional cohesiveness – to allow such isolation to continue. Often thought of as a disadvantage, Neosho should use its small size as an asset, in pursuit of a unified, close-knit center of learning, in which the different levels would assist one another. That was not the case at the time of this study, due in large part to the unwillingness of both the elementary and high school staffs to meet outside of regular school hours. Although such meetings are difficult to maintain on a regular basis, they are nonetheless crucial to the future success of the school system and vital to its efficient operation. This opportunity is not available in the larger school systems of Indianapolis, Gary, or Fort Wayne, for example; sheer numbers often prevent multi-level interaction in these places. To an outsider, one might even consider the concept of regular communication to be innate to the small-town school. Thus, it is very surprising that little is known of the day-to-day operations between the two schools in Neosho.

Improved transmission of course materials at the end of the school year. Although this would not make an immediate impact on curriculum development, it would nonetheless provide stability for new staff members who arrive each year and for veteran teachers who are changing their teaching areas. This concept may be attained by introducing more stringent requirements for end-of-the-year teacher checkout, such as the official submission of unit plans, lesson modules, or other items used that would be helpful to potential replacements.   Over the summer months, these plans could be combined into different *thematic* units.

   Careful examination of previous curricular reform efforts. This strategy had already been commenced by Dr. Allen, and he planned to incorporate past reform efforts into subsequent faculty meetings in the coming year. In addition to re-enabling documents that the older faculty had once created, this process would also be helpful to younger teachers, who can see both the process and product of curriculum development for the first time.   One of the larger frustrations of the faculty was the disposal of such efforts in the past; careful examination of these efforts would allow these efforts to "come to life" once again, and serve some use for Neosho's curricular needs in contemporary times.

   Improved preparation in curricular issues at teacher-educating colleges and universities.   Nearly all of the younger teachers conveyed trepidation about participating in curricular reform.   While much of this fear may be due to a lack of experience, colleges and universities that are preparing teachers should nonetheless address this area more fervently.   Few such institutions offer – much less require – a course in curriculum for undergraduates.   With curriculum being at the core of a practicing teacher's profession, topics regarding its construction, execution, and revision must be engaged at the pre-service level. If left ignored, the consequences (as witnessed at Neosho, with most of the staff having less than three years experience) can be severe.   It is probable that colleges and universities do not sense the curricular hardships of school systems such as Neosho, as the topic of "curriculum" is complex and confusing, as well as different in content and use from place to place. However, institutions of higher education have a responsibility to see that their graduates are carefully informed in this regard and are prepared to participate in the most basic of curricular discussions upon assuming their first jobs in American schools.

   Furthermore, it may be helpful to "de-departmentalize" the school in conceiving new curricular strategies.   Nachtigal (1992) suggests that "rural schools could lead the way in the development of a more effective curriculum" through a transformation of its academic departments into interdisciplinary teams (p. 81). As small as Neosho High School is – with its largest department possessing three members – it can be counterproductive to keep these strict divisions of academic content.   Ideas such as team-teaching may serve great benefit, in an effort to take advantage of the small department sizes at the school.

In a more specific sense, there is another possibility for improvement of the curricular dialogue at Neosho. The school system could form a working partnership with a nearby institution of higher education in an effort to revive these discussions, such as in the Professional Development School (PDS) format. As noted previously, the small rural school has been typically disconnected from the curricular resources of higher education (Schmidt, et al., 1994; Moriarity, 1981). The town is within close proximity of several colleges and universities, and a mutual benefit could result in such a partnership. For instance, in return for accepting a large contingent of student teachers from the cooperating university, Neosho could receive the assistance of university faculty in producing a new curriculum. The student teachers could be specially selected for this project and participate in the curriculum development process themselves. Such an environment would set a good example for the rest of the faculty at Neosho, who have encountered difficulty in enlisting the input of younger teachers in the curriculum design process. This program may also encourage gifted, young teachers to consider working in rural areas, whereas in the past, they may have pursued only the more lucrative urban and suburban jobs. Once a basis of trust is established between the school system and the university, the benefits of the relationship can grow exponentially over a period of years.

Summary

The results and conclusions from this study can be used by the general public to learn about the inner-workings of a small, rural high school. However, it is the greater hope of the author that this study will also be used by teachers, administrators, and townspeople of rural America for their own self-examination. This study has shown that, despite diminutive size and personnel numbers, frequent and fluent communication may not always be present in small schools. Thus, the fact that a school is "small" – either indigenously or through a de-centralization campaign – will not guarantee that quality communication takes place among its staff. Communication, like any product of human existence, must come from within the teachers themselves. An atmosphere of open communication is not conferred from on high; rather, it is developed through the persistent efforts of individuals, who envision its role in the long-term success of an organization. In other words, although good communication can be encouraged, it cannot be coerced; the people involved must desire to have it. Furthermore, when one considers the history of rural school curriculum (as examined previously), it is evident that all rural schools and rural areas do not have the same culture; educational policy and strategies must be interpretable locally in order to be effective.

Many peripheral factors influenced the Neosho teachers' desires to participate in curricular discussion, as well as the components they wished to see in a new curriculum. The teachers at Neosho are among the lowest-paid in the public schools of Indiana; these teachers also worked without a contract for the 1997-98 school year. In working at one of the smallest high schools in the state, the teachers at Neosho were also asked to undertake a variety of extra-curricular duties – regardless of whether they were willing or qualified to do so. Due to a lack of available substitutes, the principal himself was forced to instruct in the place of an absent teacher, while attempting to complete his other duties. The teachers generally maintained a deep-rooted disrespect for the local school board. They perceived the board representatives to be inflexible, unimaginative, and even uneducated.

While these factors may appear marginal to the concept of curriculum, they are certainly interwoven into the daily fabric of the school life. Consequently, they indeed become part of the "enacted" curriculum, as discussed in the Introduction to this book. The curriculum, as passed down in the school board/school office/classroom chain, can change drastically through the attitudes, experiences, and values of the individuals involved.

When considering a topic as important as curriculum, a small, rural school system must not assume that it has the advantage of a close-knit teaching staff. As shown in this study, two or three individuals that comprise an academic department may have no idea what each other is doing in their classrooms. Care must be taken in providing forums for curricular discussion. As noted earlier, this discussion cannot be forced; however, *opportunities* for discussion must be present, as little initiative may otherwise be taken to do this important work.

12. Conclusions and Thoughts for the Future

A little neglect may breed great mischief; for without a nail the shoe is lost, without a shoe the horse is lost, and without a horse the rider is lost.

– Benjamin Franklin

The story of Neosho – true and fully told – is but one ethnography among the cast of thousands in American rural schools over the past centuries. The traits, personalities, and customs of the Neosho community cannot be generalized to all rural places, but viewing such a place gives a certain degree of insight to the inner-workings of those like it. Concepts such as the value placed on local school control, the traditions of the community, and the impact of "outsiders" can be seen in all such places – in various flavors. Neosho is also but one lone reflection on the history of rural curriculum presented earlier in this book – and it, like all schools in our nation, serves to compliment an entire, vivid portrait of our educational values structure.

As was the case nationwide in the early 1900s, such was the case in Indiana in late 1900s; governmental and bureaucratic forces could not force collective change on individual school systems, no matter how well-intended the outcomes. Public education in the United States has remained, and most likely will continue to be, a matter of local control. While not purposeful saboteurs, the residents of rural America employ what educational philosopher Donald Erickson referred to as "creative insubordination" – the translated use of standardized policy and practice in a way that is practical for a given locality. In other words, rural residents have long been told how to live their lives, and how to prepare their young people for adulthood; but instead, they have proceeded with their own tried-and-true measures in each individual place, and the results have been beneficial in most cases – at least for local need.

There has been a growing trend in recent years of people returning to the rural American small town – or arriving there for the first time. Urban vices of crime and congestion have led many to restart their personal lives in the country. Often, however, the professional component of these peoples' lives remain in the city; for this is where the employment opportunities continue. The lower cost of living in rural areas attracts homebuyers, but many business investors are wary of the marketability of taking their goods and services to less populated areas.

The important problem for the future of rural communities, then, is this: will the "new populace" of rural areas – that is, those who live but do not work in a given community – grow to have vested interests in these areas, and in particular, vested interests in the local schools? One would think that people would indeed be vested in the local schools if their children attended those schools, wherever they may be; but are *families* moving to the countryside, or are these simply people looking to escape the high taxes of the city? As seen in Neosho, even teachers in many rural communities choose not to live where they work. Should only teachers, police officers, and other public figures be expected to do so?

Education is often dominated by the pulleys of control. Local communities seek a balance between controlling their own schools and enlisted state and national support, while governmental agencies try to help local areas without the appearance of "being controlling." What results in most cases, at least in rural areas, is little control and little help from the overseers; for even at the state level, little can be done to assist Neosho if the residents and schools personnel won't implement a change, nor can little control be exerted by the state to implement a change that it deems important. The government cannot clean up the trash in an urban neighborhood if the residents will not keep it clean; nor can the government install improvements in rural schools if the communities are not open to change.

There needs to be a reaffirmation by the American public of the need for strong rural places, as well as the right of rural students to study subjects interesting and particular to them. Long ago, Betts (1913) envisioned one of two unenviable outcomes from a lack of such a spirit. "If the curriculum contains no subject matter related to the immediate experience and occupation of the pupil, his education is certain to entice him away from his old interests and activities. The farm boy whose studies lack all point of contact with his life will soon either lose interest in the curriculum or turn his back on the farm" (p. 61). In the twenty-first century, reports vary as to the aspirations of young people from rural areas; some claim that they are returning to their hometowns in droves, while other statistics claim that they are yet heading to the cities in great numbers.

Since the Founding Fathers drafted the paperwork for the governance of society, the United States has been generally able to strike a balance between national/state regulation and local autonomy. Townships, communities, neighborhoods, sprawling suburbs, and big cities all reap the benefits and engage the responsibilities of this balance. It is up to the local residents to see that their own streets are kept clean; no one else can clean them, nor tell the residents to pour garbage on them.

A balance not so easily struck, however, has been the production of an American citizenry that is both nationalistic and localized in its character and pride. The curriculum – the instrument that many use for social change (not just educators, but concerned citizens of all walks of life) – has indeed been the ultimate political football. It is moved briskly "downfield" with momentum from one "team." Suddenly, though, the momentum stops and the team must punt, as another team gets its chance to "move the ball." As Kliebard called the modern American curriculum the product of an "untidy compromise," the teams on the field have played to essentially a zero-zero tie.

At the heart of much contemporary curriculum-making is the broadly-defined concept of Discovery Learning, with sub-genres such as the Problem-Based approach, the Project-Based approach, and many others. It is designed with the premise of knowing not *what to learn*, but *how to learn*. A catch-phrase seen plastered in the hallways of many schools is the pursuit of "life-long learning" for the students; that, with the advent of the Information Age, students need to sift through the mountains of data to find what is most useful. Furthermore (it is argued by some)... how is a teacher supposed to make wise selections for a modern-day curriculum, in an academic year that is still roughly 180 days long, with the ever-expanding body of knowledge that is set before them?

Today's teachers, school principals, and educators of all kinds must be careful not to become frustrated and throw out all traditional curriculum, simply because there is too much to choose from, or because it has become fashionable to label rote learning as boring; for as a recent competition by the National Geographic Society noted, 85% of American high school students in 2002 did not know where Afghanistan was on a world map – even after the murderous terrorist attacks on our soil that originated from that country. In another example of our abandonment of traditional learning, the author of this book recently spoke to a group of 43 high seniors, and not one could tell him the years in which the American Civil War took place. This is very disturbing, and evidence of the fact that the traditional curriculum – with yes, all of its supposedly boring memorization of fact – should still maintain a crucial place in our teaching today. While those who like to call themselves "educational progressives" see fact memorization as too unentertaining for students, the author fears the day when Americans forget their entire heritage, let alone their times tables – simply because teachers were made to feel that they had to compete with MTV for students attention with learning methods that were more "fun." The fact is that students need fact; if for nothing else, for the ability to communicate their culture and history to the next generation.

Epilogue

As the 2002-2003 school year came to a close, not much had changed in Neosho – except for the teaching roster, of course. Only four of the nineteen teachers remain from the 1997-1998 school year when this study was conducted. This was to be expected, as history had displayed a consistent turnover in nearly every year. The superintendent of the district has remained the same, but yet another principal sits in the main office, as that position has remained in a permanent state of attrition as well.

The demographic population of the student body had not changed much in five years; the high school students were 99% Caucasian, while nearly one-fifth (19%) of the students received either free or reduced-cost lunch. The ISTEP continues to be the measuring stick for scholastic efficacy in the state, and the percentage of students at Neosho passing the test was above the state average at the end of this study in 1998 (71% to 66%); in 2002, the Neosho students were exactly at the state average (67%), after a steep decline in 2001 (53% to 67%). In specific subject areas of the ISTEP, the students at Neosho were slightly above the state average among those passing the English/Language Arts portion (73% to 68%), while slightly below the state average in Math (66% to 63%). The numbers in Math were somewhat alarming, in light of the fact that Neosho students were significantly above the state average in this subject at

Appendix

Graduation Requirements for [Neosho,] Indiana High School

Regular Diploma

A total of 40 credits are required to graduate from Neosho High School. The basic requirements are as follows. College bound students are to note the high school credits required for admission to college discussed later in this section.

English	8 credits
Mathematics	4 credits
Science	4 credits
U.S. History	2 credits
U.S. Government	1 credit
Economics, Sociology, or Psychology	1 credit
* Health	1 credit
Physical Education	1 credit
Elective Courses	18 credits

*   The Home Economics option may be taken to replace this requirement.

Academic Honors Diploma

A total of 47 credits are required to receive the Academic Honors Diploma. Course requirements for this diploma are as follows:

English   8 credits

Mathematics   8 credits
    (Algebra 1 and 2, Geometry, Advanced Math)

Science   6 credits
            (Biology 1 and 2, Chemistry, Physics or Earth Science)

Social Studies   6 credits
            (U.S. History and Government, Economics, Geography or
            World History)

Foreign Language   6 credits of one
                        language or 4 credits each in two areas

Fine Arts   2 credits
(art, band, music, or art appreciation)

* Health   1 credit
Physical Education   1 credit
Elective Courses

No grade lower than a "C" may count towards these credits

* The Home Economics option may be taken to replace this requirement.

Entrance Requirements for Indiana Colleges and Universities

Students who enter the 9th grade in the fall of 1994 and [*sic*] after must meet the following curricular requirements in order to be considered for admission to Indiana's four-year public institutions. The same curriculum is recommended for those seeking admission to Indiana's two-year public institutions.

Language Arts   8 credits in literature, composition, and
speech

Mathematics   6-8 credits from the following courses:
                                        Algebra 1
                                        Geometry
                                        Algebra 2
                                        Trigonometry
                                        Calculus

Science	6 credits in the following laboratory courses: 2 in Biology 2 in Chemistry or Physics 2 in Advanced Biology, Chemistry, Physics, or Earth/Space Science
Social Studies	6 credits in the following courses: 2 in U.S. History, 1 in U.S. Government, 1 in Economics 1 in World History and/or Geography; 1 additional course from above or other social studies area
Directed Electives	8 credits of additional courses in the above subject areas, or: Foreign Language, Fine Arts, Computer Applications, Technical Career Preparation

Effective in the fall of 1994, the public post-secondary institutions offered preferred admission to recipients of the Academic Honors Diploma who achieve at least a "B" average grade in their required academic courses.

Effective in the fall of 1994, the public post-secondary institutions will implement early admission arrangements for high school students who have completed the curricular requirements for admission consideration and meet other institutional admission requirements prior to receiving high school diplomas.

Class Load

Students may sign up for one study hall. If students must be removed from class due to academic or behavior problems, they will be suspended from school attendance and recommended for expulsion unless they are enrolled in a minimum of four subjects.

Class Standing

To be classified as a "sophomore," a student must have earned 9 credits and have completed 2 semesters in high school. To be classified as a "junior," a student must have earned 18 credits and have completed 4 semesters in high school. To be classified as a "senior," a student must have earned 27 credits and have completed 6 semesters in high school.
([Neosho], Indiana Consolidated School Corporation, 1998)

The fact that the school offers an "Academic Honors" diploma option introduces a curricular difficulty. Of the various courses stipulated under this section, the availability of several were contingent upon minimum enrollments. According to teachers in different departments within the high school, if such enrollments are not attained, interested students must pursue a telecourse option – which may or may not be available in a given semester. This option (if present) involves the student watching a course being taught at another location, without interaction with that location. Thus, the courses that a student would take in this honors program would differ from traditional practices, perhaps altering the experience in either a positive or negative way.

Course Offerings and Enrollment at Neosho High School, 1996-97

Subject	Students
1st Year Biology, General	33
1st Year Chemistry, General	13
1st Year Earth/Space Science, General	34
1st Year Physics, General	2
2nd Year Chemistry, General	6

Accounting, Advanced	3
Accounting, Beginning	15
Advanced Physical Education	18
Advanced Three-Dimensional Art	1
Advanced Two-Dimensional Art	4
Algebra, 1st Year	43
Algebra, 2nd Year	12
Animal Science	5
Art	32
Art Appreciation	1
Auto Mechanics	2
Band (all levels)	19
Basic Physical Education	44
Body and Fender Repair	1
Chemistry/Physics Lab	1
Computer Applications	15
Computer Literacy	16
Consumer Education	16
Economics	14
Electronics	1
English	50
English 9	41
English 10	37
English 11	31
English 12	28
Family Management	12
Farm Management	6
Food Science	14
Food and Nutrition I	16
Food and Nutrition II	6
Fundamentals of Agricultural Science	32
General Home Economics	15
General Mathematics	11
General Science	13
Geometry	28
Health Education	74
Word Processing	10
Introduction to Communications Technology	10
Introduction to Construction Technology	6
Introduction to Health Careers	1

Introduction to Industrial Technology	33
Introduction to Manufacturing Technology	107
Introduction to Three-Dimensional Art	8
Introduction to Two-Dimensional Art	29
Learning Disabled	25
Mathematics	30
Advanced Placement Mathematics	3
Physical Education	17
Pre-Algebra	35
Science	65
Social Studies	65
Sociology	7
Spanish I	44
Spanish II	12
Spanish III	6
Spanish IV	3
Speech	13
Trigonometry	4
United States Government	20
United States History (20th Century)	34
Woods	14
World Geography	18
World History / Civilization	22

(Indiana Department of Education, 1998)

References

Apple, M. (1975). The hidden curriculum and the nature of conflict. From *Curriculum Theorizing* (Pinar, Ed.).

Asplaugh, J. (1992). Socioeconomic measures and achievement: Urban vs. rural. *Rural Educator, 13* (3), 2-7.

Bachus, G. (1992). School-based management: Do teachers want more involvement in decision making? *Rural Educator, 14* (1), 1-4.

Bainer, D. (1997). A comparison of four models of group efforts and their implications for establishing educational partnerships. *Journal of Research in Rural Education, 13* (3), 143-152.

Barker, B. (1990). Distance education in rural schools: Advantages and disadvantages. *Rural Educator, 12* (1), 4-7.

Barker, B. & Hall, R. (1998). Planning for technology implementation in rural schools. *Rural Educator, 19* (3), 1-6.

Baumeister, M. & Morris, R. (1992). Rural delivery model for vocational education. *Teaching Exceptional Children, 24* (4), 40-43.

Beaumont, R. (1995). Start the presses! *Executive Educator, 17* (12), 26-27.

Bennett, W. (1992). *The de-valuing of America: The fight for our culture and our children.* New York: Simon and Schuster.

Benson, C. (1996). Good country practice: Put the horse before the cart, and curriculum before assessment. *Education Week, 15* (17), 32.

Beyer, L. & Liston, D. (1996). *Curriculum in conflict: Social visions, educational agendas, and progressive school reform.* New York: Teachers College Press.

Betts, G. (1913). *New ideals in rural schools.* Boston: Houghton Mifflin.

Biklen, S. & Bogden, R. (1982). *Qualitative research for education: An introduction to theory and methods.* Boston: Allyn and Bacon.

Blanchard, C. (1884). *Counties of Morgan, Monroe, and Brown, Indiana: Historical and biographical.* Chicago: F.A. Battey and Company.

Bloom, A. (1987). *The closing of the American mind.* Riverside, NJ: Simon and Schuster.

Bobbitt, F. (1918). *The curriculum.* Boston: Houghton.

Bobbitt, F. (1920a). *How to make a curriculum.* Boston: Houghton.

Bobbitt, F. (1920b). The objectives of secondary education. *The School Review, 28* (10), 738-749.

Bobbitt, F. (1925). Difficulties to be met in local curriculum-making. *Elementary School Journal, 25,* 653-663.

Boone, M. (1998). Instructional leadership practices of small, rural school district superintendents. *Rural Educator, 19* (3), 15-19.

Borg, W. & Gall, M. (1989). *Educational research: An introduction.* White Plains, NY: Longman.

Brameld, T. (1971). *Patterns of educational philosophy: Divergence and convergence in culturological perspective.* New York: Holt, Rinehart, and Winston.

Brown, D. & others (1996). Principals' perceptions of community and staff involvement in shared decision making. *Journal of Research in Rural Education, 12* (1), 17-24.

Burton,W. & Barnes, W. (1929). *The supervision of elementary subjects.* New York: Appleton.

Bussis, A., & others (1976). *Beyond surface curriculum: An interview study of teachers' understandings.* Boulder, CO: Westview Press.

Butler, N. M. (1894). The reform of secondary education in the United States. *Atlantic Monthly, 73,* 372-384.

Butterworth, J. & Dawson, H. (1952). *The modern rural school.* New York: McGraw-Hill.

Chamberlin, D. & others (1942). *Did they succeed in college? The follow-up study of the graduates of the thirty schools* (Volume Four). New York: Harper and Brothers.

Charters, W. (1923). *Curriculum construction.* Columbus: The Ohio State University.

Church, S. (1988). It's almost like there aren't any walls... . *Language Arts, 65* (5), 448-454.

Clandinin, J. & Connelly, M. (1992). Teacher as curriculum maker. From *The Handbook of Research on Curriculum,* 363-401.

Clarke, J. & Hood, K. (1986). School improvement in a rural state. *Educational Leadership, 44* (1), 77-80.

Conant, J. (1959). *The American high school today: A first report to interested citizens.* New York: McGraw-Hill.

Conant, J. (1963). *The education of American teachers.* New York: McGraw-Hill.

Conant, J. (1967). *The comprehensive high school: A second report to interested citizens.* New York: McGraw-Hill.

Counts, G. (1932). *Dare the school build a new social order?* New York: John Day.

Counts, G. (1952). *Education and American civilization*. New York: Teachers College Bureau of Publications.

Cubberly, E. (1912). *The improvement of rural schools*. Boston: Houghton-Mifflin.

Davis, O.L. (1977). The nature and boundaries of curriculum history. *Curriculum Inquiry, 7* (2), 157-168.

DeGarmo, C. (1896). *Herbart and the Herbartians*. New York: Charles Scribner's Sons Publications.

Dewey, J. (1922). *Human nature and conduct*. New York: Modern Library.

Dewey, J. (1938). *Experience and education*. New York: Collier Books.

Dunne, F. (1982). Activism comes to Iowa Falls, Iowa. From *Rural Education: In Search of a Better Way*. Boulder, CO: Westivew Press.

Eckman, J. (2000). Busing hearings in West Virginia: Citizens tell their tales. *Rural Policy Matters, 2* (2), 1-8.

Eisner, E. (1990). Creative curriculum development and practice. *Journal of Curriculum and Supervision, 6* (1), 62-73.

Eliot, C. (1894). The unity of educational reform. *Educational Review, 8* (7), 209-226.

Eliot, C. (1908). Industrial education as an essential factor in our national prosperity. In *Bulletin Number Five of the National Society for the Promotion of Industrial Education*. New York: The Society.

Feldmann, D. (2000). National policy, local interpretation: The American rural curriculum, 1897-1921. *Rural Educator, 21* (1), 8-14.

Finney, R. (1928). *A sociological philosophy of education.* New York: Macmillan.

Fleming, L. (1995). Consolidation comes to Ashland County, Ohio. *Midwestern Educational Researcher, 8* (4), 25-27.

Friedberger, M. (1996). Country schooling in the heartland. *American Journal of Education, 104* (2), 148-153.

Fuller, W. (1982). *The old country school: The story of rural education in the Middle West.* Chicago: The University of Chicago Press.

Fuller, W. (1994). *One-room schools of the Middle West.* Lawrence, KS: University Press of Kansas.

Gardener, C. (1984). A survey of rural schools in Montana. *Rural Educator, 5* (2), 18-21.

Giroux, H. (1983). *Theory and resistance in education: A pedagogy for the opposition.* South Hadley, MA: Bergin and Garvey.

Glen, M. (1980). Curriculum planning in a Queensland one-teacher school. *Forum for the Discussion of New Trends in Education, 23* (1), 25-26.

Goodlad, J. (1969). Curriculum: State of the field. *Review of Educational Research, 39* (3), 367-375.

Gregory, T. & Smith, G. (1987). *High schools as communities: The small school reconsidered.* Bloomington, IN: Phi Delta Kappa.

Hadley, M. & Wood, R. (1987). Integrating international education into rural schools. *Rural Educator, 9* (1), 15-18.

Haller, E. & Monk, D. (1988). New reforms, old reforms, and the consolidation of small rural schools. *Educational Administration Quarterly, 24* (4), 470-483.

Harris, W. T. (1880). *Equivalents in a liberal course of study.* Journal of Proceeding and Addresses of the National Education Association Annual Meeting, 169-175.

Harris, W. T. (1895). *Report of the Committee of Fifteen: Correlation of studies in elementary schools.* Boston: New England Publishing Company.

Harris, W.T. (1898). The pedagogical creed of William T. Harris, U.S. Commissioner of Education. In O.H. Lang (Ed.), *Educational Creeds of the Nineteenth Century.* New York: E.L. Kellogg.

Herzog, M. & Pittman, R. (1995). Home family, and community: Ingredients in the rural education equation. *Phi Delta Kappan, 77* (2), 113-118.

Hirsch, E.D. (1987). *Cultural literacy: What every American needs to know.* Boston: Houghton-Mifflin.

Hirsch, E.D. (1996). *The schools we need and why we don't have them.* Boston: Houghton-Mifflin.

Holloway, W. (1928). *Participation in curriculum planning as a means of supervision in rural schools.* New York: Teachers College Press.

Hutto, N. (1990). Rural schools can be effective schools, too! *Rural Educator, 11* (3), 6-9.

Illinois State Board of Education (2001). Internet Site: http://www.isbe.state.il.us.

Indiana Department of Education (1998 and 2002). Internet Site. http://ideanet.doe.state.in.us.

Indiana General Assembly (1998). *Burns' Indiana Statutes.* Indianapolis: Indiana State Government.

Jackson, P. (1990). Looking for trouble: On the place of the ordinary in educational studies. From *Qualitative Inquiry in Education: The Continuing Debate.* New York: Teachers College Press.

Joiner, L. & others (1981). Independent study: Route to academic equity for rural high schools. *Educational Leadership, 38* (7), 578-580.

Kaestle, C. (1983). *Pillars of the republic: Common schools and American society.* New York: Hill and Wang.

Kannapel, P. & others (1995). Six heads are better than one? School-based decision making in rural Kentucky. *Journal of Research in Rural Education, 11* (1), 15-23.

Kilpatrick, W. (1936). *Remaking the curriculum.* New York: Newson and Company.

Kirst, M. & Walker, D. (1971). An analysis of curriculum policy-making. *Review of Educational Research, 41* (5), 479-509.

Kliebard, H. (1975). Persistent curriculum issues in historical perspective. From *Curriculum Theorizing* (Pinar, Ed.).

Kliebard, H. (1995a). *The struggle for the American curriculum.* New York: Routledge.

Kliebard, H. (1995b). The Cardinal Principles report as archeological deposit. *Curriculum Studies, 3* (2) 197-208.

Kliebard, H. (1998). The effort to reconstruct the modern American curriculum. From *The Curriculum: Problems, Prospects, and Possibilities.* New York: SUNY Press.

Leidecker, K. (1946). *Yankee teacher: The life of William Torrey Harris.* New York: Philosophical Library.

Leight, R. & Rinehart, A. (1992). Revisiting Americana: One-room school in retrospect. *Educational Forum, 56* (2), 133-151.

Longstreet, W. & Shane, H. (1993). *Curriculum for the new millennium.* Boston: Allyn and Bacon.

Lovelady, I. (1992). The day the mill closed. *Educational Leadership, 50* (1), 55-56.

Lundgren, R. (1985). Two-way television in rural curriculum development. *NASSP Bulletin, 69* (484), 15-19.

Manges, C. & Wilcox, D. (1997). The role of the principal in rural school reform. *Rural Educator, 18* (3), 21-23.

Mann, H. (1848). *The twelfth annual report* [on common schools]. Boston: Massachusetts State Assembly.

Martin, D. (1998). Gymnasium or coliseum? Basketball, education, and community impulse in Indiana in the early twentieth century. From *Hoosier Schools, Past and Present.* Bloomington, IN: Indiana University Press.

Massey, S. & Crosby, J. (1983). Special problems, special opportunities: Preparing teachers for rural schools. *Phi Delta Kappan, 65* (4), 265-269.

Matranga, M. & others (1995). Working with high-risk youth: A collaborative approach. *Journal of Extension, 33* (3),

Maxwell, W. H. (1894). The committee of ten. *Journal of Education, 39* (10), 153.

McCracken, J. & Miller, C. (1988). Rural teachers' perceptions of their schools and communities. *Research in Rural Education, 5* (2), 23-26.

McIntire, W. & others (1990). Rural school counselors: Their communities and schools. *School Counselor, 37* (3), 166-172.

McMurry, C. (1901). *The elements of general method based on the principles of Herbart.* Bloomington, IL: Public School Publishing Company.

Mirel, J. & Angus, D. (1994). High standards for all? The struggle for equality in the American high school curriculum, 1890-1990. *American Educator, 18,* 4-9.

Moriarity, T. (1981). Problems of rural superintendents in western South Dakota. *Rural Educator, 3* (1), 1-5.

Nachtigal, P. (1982). *Rural education: In search of a better way.* Boulder, CO: Westview Press.

Nachtigal, P. (1992). Secondary education. From *Education in the Rural Community.* Malabar, FL: Krieger Publishing.

Nachitgal, P. & Theobald, P. (1995). Culture, community, and the promise of rural education. *Phi Delta Kappan, 77* (2), 132-135.

National Commission on Excellence in Education (1983). *A nation at risk: The Imperative for educational reform.* Washington, D.C.: U.S. Government Printing Office.

National Education Association (1893). *Report of the committee on secondary school Studies* [Committee of Ten]. Washington, D.C.: United States Government Printing Office.

National Education Association (1897-1921). *Journal of Proceedings and Addresses.*

National Society for the Study of Education (1914). *Annual Yearbook.*

Odden, E. & Wohlstetter, P. (1995). Making school-based management work. *Educational Leadership, 52* (5), 32-36.

Ornstein, A. & Hunkins, F. (1988). *Curriculum: Foundations, principles, and issues.* New York: Prentice-Hall.

Page, D. (1849). *Theory and practice of teaching: Or, the motives and methods of good school-keeping.* New York: A.S. Barnes Company.

Parker, F.W. (1894). *Talks on pedagogics.* Chicago: University of Chicago Press.

Parker, F.W. (1899). The child. *National Education Association Journal of Proceedings and Addresses,* p. 482.

Parker, F.W. (1902). *The Quincy Method.* Report of the Commissioner of Education for the year 1902. Washington: U.S. Bureau of Education.

Peshkin, A. (1978). *Growing up American: Schooling and the survival of community.* Chicago: University of Chicago Press.

Peshkin, A. (1992). The relationship between culture and curriculum: A many fitting thing. From *The Handbook of Research on Curriculum,* 248-267.

Pinar, W. and others (1995). *Understanding curriculum.* New York: Peter Lang.

Porter, M. (1996). Moving mountains: Reform, resistance, and resiliency in an Appalachian Kentucky high school. *Rural Educator, 18* (2), 25-29.

Powell, N. (1991). School-based management in smaller secondary schools. *NASSP Bulletin, 75* (533), 11-15.

Pratt, D. (1980). *Curriculum: Design and development.* New York: Harcourt Brace Jovanovich.

Rippa, S.A. (1992). *Education in a free society.* New York: Longman.

Rugg, H. (1938). *Our country and our people: An introduction to American civilization.* Boston: Ginn.

Queitzsch, M. & Nelson, S. (1996). An assessment of priorities and constraints: Curriculum renewal in small rural school districts. *Rural Educator, 18* (2), 17-19, 24.

Sadker, D. & Sadker, M. (1988). *Teachers, schools, and society.* New York: Random House.

Schaffarzich, J. (1976). *Current issues, problems, and concerns in curriculum development.* Washington: National Institute of Education, Task Force on Curriculum Development.

Schmidt, K. and others (1994). Teaching migrant students algebra by audioconference. *American Journal of Distance Education, 8* (3), 51-63.

Schubert, W. (1980). *Curriculum books: The first eighty years.* Washington, D.C.: University Press of America.

Schwandt, T. (1997). *Qualitative inquiry: A dictionary of terms.* Thousand Oaks, CA: Sage Publications.

Seal, K. & Harmon, H. (1995). Realities of rural school reform. *Phi Delta Kappan, 77* (2), 119-124.

Shaw, G. (1991). Small and rural schools must unite for representation. *NASSP Bulletin, 75* (533), 17-21.

Sher, J. (1983). Bringing home the bacon: The politics of rural school reform. *Phi Delta Kappan, 65* (4), 279-283.

Sher, J. (1995). The battle for the soul of rural school reform. *Phi Delta Kappan, 77* (2), 143-148.

Siegmund, D. & McFadden, J. (1985). Linking smaller schools for a more effective curriculum. *NASSP Bulletin, 69* (484), 35-38.

Small, R. (1977). Censorship, schools, and textbooks. *Kappa Delta Pi Record, 13* (4), 125-127.

Snedden, D. (1921). *Sociological determination of objectives in education.* Philadelphia: J.B. Lippincott Company.

Spring, J. (1986). *The American school, 1642-1985.* New York: Longman.

Theobald, P. (1993). Country school curriculum and governance: The one-room school experience in the nineteenth-century Midwest. *American Journal of Education, 101* (2), 116-139.

Theobald, P. (1995). *Call school: Rural education in the Midwest to 1918.* Carbondale, IL: Southern Illinois University Press.

Tyler, R. (1949). *Basic principles of curriculum and instruction.* Chicago: University of Chicago Press.

Tyree, C. (1996). Collaboration and empowerment: A prescription for rural school education. *Rural Educator, 17* (2), 14-17.

Uhl, P. & others (1993). Barriers to school-based management. *Rural Educator, 14* (3), 4-6.

Uhrmacher, F.B. (1997). The curriculum shadow. *Curriculum Inquiry, 27* (3), 317-329.

Urban, W. and Waggoner, J. (1996). *American education: A history.* New York: McGraw-Hill.

United States Congress (1958). *National Defense Education Act.* Washington, D.C.: United States Government.

United States Department of Commerce (1999). *Economics and statistics administration: Bureau of the census.* Washington, D.C.: United States Government.

United States Department of Education (2000). *Digest of Education Statistics.* Washington, D.C.: United States Government.

Wall, L. & others (1991). Schools as entrepeneurs: Helping small towns survive. *Rural Educator, 12* (3), 16-20.

Weiler, K. (1994). Women and rural school reform: California, 1900-1940. *History of Education Quarterly, 34* (1), 25-47.

Willis, G. & others (1994). *The American curriculum: A documentary history.* Westport, CT: Praeger.

Wolcott, H. (1994). *Transforming qualitative data: Description, analysis, and interpretation.* Thousand Oaks, CA: Sage Publications.

Worthy, W. (1988). College chemistry to be offered via satellite to rural high schools. *Chemical and Engineering News, 66* (36), 15-16.

Yoder, J. (1985). Gifted education is for rural students, too. *NASSP Bulletin, 69* (482), 68-74.

Zellermayer, M. (1997). When we talk about collaborative curriculum-making, what are we talking about? *Curriculum Inquiry, 27* (2), 187-213.

Index

About the Author

Doug Feldmann (Ph.D., Indiana University) has devoted much of the research portion of his academic career to the study of curriculum theory and rural education. In addition to various journal articles on educational topics, Dr. Feldmann is also the author of three other books, all of which deal with baseball history and the sociological effect of the sport on urban and small-town America: *Dizzy and the Gas House Gang, Fleeter Than Birds,* and *The 1935 Chicago Cubs* (all published by McFarland and Company). Dr. Feldmann resides in Indianapolis, and is a professor of education and assistant baseball coach at Franklin College. He may be e-mailed at the following address: dfeldmann@franklincollege.edu.